I Will Bring The Colour

Ingrid's Story

I Will Bring The Colour

Ingrid's Story

INGRID AND MARY WALSH

ISBN 978-1-80352-715-4

Text Ingrid and Mary Walsh
Copyright © Mary Walsh

Text is Private and confidential

First Print April 2023

ISBN 978-1-80352-715-4

9 781803 527154 >

CONTENTS

FOREWORD BY 'INGRID'S MAM'

"Someone forgot to tell me that I was not supposed to live"
Ingrid Walsh

Most people know me as 'Ingrid's mam'. It is a title I am beyond proud of because my daughter, Ingrid, was an inspiration to more people in this world than I will ever know.

When Ingrid started writing her story, she would tell everyone that she would only be happy if it was launched live on the Late, Late Show (preferably by Gay Byrne but she wouldn't have minded Pat Kenny or Ryan Tubridy…).

She was confident that she would eventually finish writing her story and had no doubt it would be captivating enough to enchant and inspire people in equal measure. Well Ingrid, I cannot promise you the Late, Late Show but think you would be very proud to see your story completed.

My inspirational, witty, sociable, straight-talking, genuine Ingrid bade farewell to this world on 21st June 2019 aged 48. Three years later, I am still receiving letters, poems, stories, emails, text messages, phone calls and visits from people who are struggling to fill the gap that Ingrid has left in their world. They miss her profoundly.

Ingrid was friends with a hugely diverse amount of people. She made lasting impressions on presidents, world- famous musicians, medical consultants and dignitaries. However, prince or pauper, Ingrid treated everyone exactly the same. 'Ingrid' means 'hero's daughter' in Norse. Ingrid's Dad, 'our rock', chose it, and it sums her up perfectly.

For many years in the medical world, Ingrid was also known by a number, a number that I will take to my grave. That number was 100242, and I honestly feel like it's ingrained in the core of my grieving heart to this day. I quoted Ingrid's medical number more times than I could count to hospital staff at the end of the phone. Ingrid, however, was never just a number. She was a light in an often-dark world, and now I like to think of her as a star in the heavens who will navigate others through difficult times.

This book is an attempt to encapsulate in words the spirit of a girl that lifted the hearts of every single person that was ever in her company. It also touches upon my family's torment as we fought tooth and nail to see justice done for our bright, articulated daughter when she suffered at the hands of a flawed system.

This battle for Ingrid took our family on a harrowing journey which eventually led to an out of court settlement of 2.5 million Euros.

I firmly believe that it was negligence and malpractice on the part of this system that stole the essence of Ingrid away 14 years before her death. All the money in the world wasn't going to change that but it is still a part of Ingrid's story that needs to be told.

However, that money ensured that our precious daughter could receive the very best care and have access to the best support for the remaining years of her life. This was the least

Ingrid deserved. And while Ingrid was not aware that I was embroiled in a legal battle, I know that she would have been proud of me. She would have looked me straight in the eye and said, "Good on you, Mam!"

That money did not take away my disappointment, anger, frustrations and strong temptation to tell the world exactly what happened to my only daughter. That temptation is still there, some days stronger than others, but I have made the wise decision not to dwell too much on that part of the story in this book.

This book is ultimately to celebrate Ingrid. I do not want to taint such a beautiful story with too many brutal truths. This book is to make readers smile and cry as they remember our precious, vivacious girl.

Today, I try my level best to stay strong and smile at the memories of both Ingrid and her wonderful father, Ernie, who passed away on 22nd July 2021.

When you have fought a lengthy battle for someone you love with all your heart, and that person dies, their legacy is all that remains, and boy does Ingrid have one of those! Ingrid's story has power beyond anything you or I can imagine. It is for this reason I want to share it, knowing in my heart of hearts that it could transform lives.

This book includes a little of my 'behind the scenes' account of life as Ingrid's mam. And while my hope is to inspire other parents to keep going and fight for their child every step of the way, I, Ingrid's Mam, am not the author of this book. I am the gap filler, the background painter, the other perspective. I have purposely chosen not to tell you why

Ingrid had a medical number or why she 'wasn't supposed to live.' I will let the author of this book, Ingrid, fill you in on that.

The truth was Ingrid's life was so colourful that everywhere she went, people urged her to write her autobiography. So, she did just that. She began putting pen to paper in earnest in 1990 at 20 years old, and you, like me, will be so glad she did.

I read her very own words now, and I can hear her witty tone once again. I close my eyes and can see her beautiful big smile. I can recall events with her, and rest assured that Ingrid had a full and happy life.

The unique 'essence' of Ingrid that we lost when she suffered a brain injury in 2005 is still in the room when I read her story. By sharing Ingrid's words with you, I hope you feel like you have spent a little bit of extra quality time with her too.

And if you never met Ingrid, I can assure you that when you read her story, you will wish you had.

To know Ingrid was to love her. It really is as simple as that.

A NOTE ON THE FORMAT OF THIS BOOK

The first chapter is, fittingly, written by Ingrid herself on the very day she decided to start writing her autobiography at 20 years old. Her words have not been changed because Ingrid was a natural storyteller and a gifted public speaker and writer. I have also not tampered with how or where in her colourful story Ingrid chose to begin because she will have had her reasons for that. You, the reader, can decide for yourself why she started where she did.

As the chapters progress, Ingrid's words are in italics and my own, in standard print.

After chapter one, the story goes back to the very beginning, when our precious child was born. Each chapter then charts her miraculous journey of surviving against the odds. It weaves its way over seemingly insurmountable peaks and plunges into challenging dark and painful valleys. However, rest assured that there are plenty of undulating, calm and joyful paths between.

Ingrid lived life to the absolute fullest right until she departed this earth. If I know Ingrid, she has kept herself busy up there in heaven preparing a perfect room filled with classical music, banter, delicious seafood and handmade chocolates for her hero, her beloved dad, who joined her just two years after her death.

Let me hand you into the most capable, caring hands of my amazing wordsmith and daughter, Ingrid...

For Luke and Ava Ingrid, in memory of Aunty Ingrid.

"Some people have the ambition to climb Everest; others want to travel the world. Writing my story is my version of climbing Everest."

Ingrid Walsh - Age 20

Ingrid

From Ingrid, a name of Norse origin,
Meaning 'hero's daughter'
She makes her own luck
Considers love the most important thing in life
Gets up every morning with enthusiasm for a new day
Views change as a fundamental law of nature and welcomes it
Always generous, never afraid to give
She never stops moving forward
A wise and patient person is what she is

With love · From Mam and Dad
Christmas 1995

1 - "THIS IS MY STORY, AND I'M STICKING TO IT..." INGRID WALSH, AGE 20

For as long as I can remember, I have been telling stories about different things that have happened throughout my life. People have been suggesting to me that I write these stories into my life story. My answer has always been, "Maybe one day, I will." That day has come! Why today? What is so special about today? Well, why not today? It is as good as any other day. Well, anyway, at last, I can say I have started and am giving myself a goal of finishing sometime in the not-too-distant future. Friends who have not seen me in a while usually ask me what I'm doing. My usual response is, "Not much." But now I can say that I am writing my autobiography, at least it sounds good!

I have always been telling people for years that we all have a story to tell, and so this is mine.

Christmas came and went. November 29th, less than a month before Christmas of 1990, everyone in the country is buzzing, everyone that is, except for me. On my way back to hospital with a mixture of uncertainty about me, for the first half of the three-hour journey, I really did not want to be heading towards Beaumont Hospital. Halfway there, my head started to ache. The pain was excruciating, and I said to Mam, "I can't see!" Mam was driving, and there were only the two of us in the car. The closer we got to the hospital, the more relieved I felt, but by the time we reached the hospital, I was screaming in agony. As we were arriving, Mr Young, the neurosurgeon I needed to see, was leaving the hospital. As soon as he saw us, he said to my Mam, "I have to collect my wife at the airport, but I will be back. Go straight to my registrar; he is waiting for you." Even though I could not see Mr Young at the time, I was delighted to hear his voice. I felt totally comfortable, even if in terrible pain, because I knew I was in the right place. The number of tests, scans, x-rays, etc. that I underwent in the next few days was mind-boggling. Finally, the day for surgery (that the medical team decided I needed) arrived. I had advised Mam not to visit me on that day. I thought this was good advice as nobody knew how long I would be in theatre.

It turned out I was in the theatre for eight hours, much longer than anyone anticipated. When I arrived back on the ward, I was wrapped in what they called a space suit. I hated having that space suit removed because I was warm in it. By the time the operation was finished, the night staff was on. Once I was returned to the high dependency ward, I thought that I could get a nice night's sleep, except for the fact that I had to be woken up for observation. There was no such thing as a night's sleep after a gruelling day in surgery.

The following day I felt as if I had gone 12 rounds with Mohammed Ali and lost. The only two things that cheered me up were the nurses looking after me (they were great!) and that I was expecting Mam and Dad to visit. When I described to the nurses how I felt, their answer was one that I will never forget. One of them told me that she had seen the fight and the other that she had seen Ali in ICU and that he was in a very bad way. Even though it hurt to laugh, it did me good. Later that day, Mam and Dad arrived. Mam came as close to the bed as she could, and she whispered in my ear, "Ingrid, are you ready for a very big surprise?" I replied in a very weak voice, "Try me." I hadn't a clue what the surprise was, and at that time, I wasn't able to think too much; I was in such pain. Mam then went out into the corridor and nodded her head. When I saw her nodding, I felt jealous because I couldn't nod if you paid me because the surgery was on the back of my neck. I only had a second to wait to find out what that surprise was. My big brother, Graham, had travelled all the way from Japan just to see me! When I saw him, I jumped up and practically disconnected every drip and tube connected to my body. Into the bargain, my pain disappeared, at least for a while. He was the best painkiller I could have asked for. Graham, my big brother, did not come empty-handed. He brought a porcelain doll, and he told me there was another, much bigger one waiting for me at home, so I had better get my skates on and get better as fast as I could.

It took me a long time to get home because my health took a nose- dive before things started improving. Things got so bad that before Christmas, I had to be brought back to the theatre to get a central line fitted. This is a drip going into your chest, a very painful procedure. But thankfully, the anaesthetist understood and completely knocked me out. So, Christmas Eve came and went, and I don't remember any of it. The following morning, Christmas morning, to be exact, it goes without saying that I was expecting my family, but I had another visitor, Mr Young, who called in to see me. He was aware of how ill I was and decided to come in and check up on me. He came straight to my bed and got down on his knees, and said two things to me. Firstly, "Merry Christmas, I know that does not mean much to you this Christmas, but next year it will." And secondly, he asked, "How are you feeling?" When I told him how much pain I was in, he moved really fast to relieve it.

That Christmas was the only one I ever saw snow on the ground. It looked like a real Christmas outside, very picturesque but a nightmare as far as I was concerned. Visitors found it very hard to travel. Although I had my family on Christmas Day, as the weather got worse, I didn't have them again until after Christmas. On 8th January, I was discharged from hospital, but there was just one slight snag; it was still snowing quite heavily, so there was no way I could be collected by my parents. Even though I had been discharged, I could not move. That afternoon, Mr Young's Senior Registrar came to see me and, in broken English, asked how I was feeling. At that stage of the day, I was feeling very sorry for myself, and when I told him, his reaction was, "That good, that very, very good." He really did not understand me, and when he left, I did not know whether to laugh or cry. My journey home started the following day; it had to be done by ambulance. The snow was still on the ground, and I was not allowed to sit up for very long periods of time. The only way I could travel was lying on a stretcher on the floor of the ambulance. Under normal circumstances, that journey would have taken approximately three hours, but because of the snow, it took two days. We had to stay overnight in Naas General Hospital and leave there early in the morning in order to get home before nightfall. Then on the way home, we had a skid *and bumped into a car driven by the Bishop of Ossory. That was the most uncomfortable and longest journey I have ever undertaken in my life.*

It is very true what they say, readers, there is definitely no place like home.

Indeed, Ingrid was so delighted to return home that she wrote a poem capturing her joy at coming back home after one of her many visits to the hospital in Dublin:

Coming Home Now

What a delight it was, when arriving home by car.
A long and painful journey from Dublin's fair city.
This journey I had to take is one I got used to, as I had
to do it regularly when I was a child.
Why you might ask was this journey necessary.
The answer always the same.
My second home the hospitals I attended.
Even though I describe these journeys as painful that pain
always left me when I reached home.
When I did reach home I faced a longer much tougher
journey. This is not a journey that I needed a car boat or
plane to undertake. No this is a journey that I must travel
under my own steam.. But not alone
far from it. There will be people I will meet along the road.
These people I know are friends and family. These people are
the reason why when the going gets tough, I feel the need to
continue my journey to the end.
What a delight it is when arriving home not far from the
bridge,
I can see the lights of Waterford city. I am over come by the
feeling that the city is alight to welcome me home.
Coming home now what a feeling.
Our house is still the same. But wait I haven't seen my room
yet. I feel quite tired so I must go
there. Nothings changed "but look closer" the room looks
brighter. Why is that? It's amazing what a lick of paint can do.

By Ingrid Walsh

So, I am sure you are wondering what on earth it is that I have going against me? Well, I was born with a disability called Spina Bifida, which is a disability of the spine.

So extreme was my condition that I was not expected to live for longer than a day but live I did... and to the fullest!

Despite my daughter describing her condition as 'going against' her, she never ever let her disability get in her way. In fact, if I close my eyes right now, I can still hear her delivering one of her favourite lines.

"I can't stand up, but I intend on standing out!" - **Ingrid Walsh**

This hugely positive attitude against all odds was typical of Ingrid. Ingrid had the most severe type of Spina Bifida that the doctors had ever seen. So severe in fact that no one before her had ever survived beyond birth.

Ingrid was never going to stand; she was never going to walk and would always be a wheelchair user.

True to her word however, Ingrid, who never stood up, certainly 'stood out' in every imaginable way throughout her life.

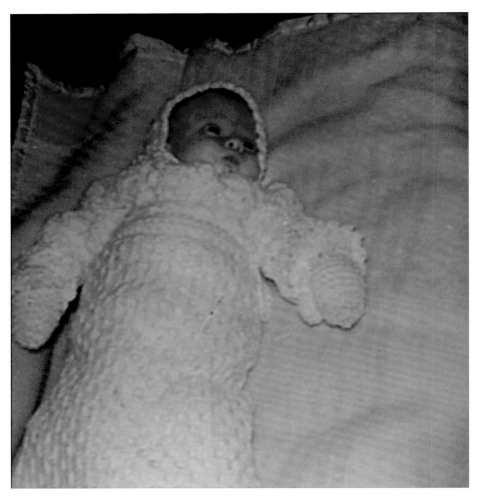

Ingrid's Christening

Ingrid's first birthday

Ingrid's second birthday

Ingrid on her christening

LEFT: with her godparents
RIGHT: with Margaret and Lucy

Ingrid with her porcelain dolls

2 - WHO AM I?

My parents are Mary and Ernest (known as Ernie) Walsh. Dad is from Carrick-on-Suir, Co. Tipperary, and Mam is from Gracedieu Road, Waterford City. They married
in 1966, and my older brother, Graham, was born in 1967. I was born in 1970, and my younger brother, Gordon, was born in 1981. I never met either of Dad's parents, as sadly, they died before I was born. His mother died in 1944 from a brain haemorrhage when Dad was only five. That was the year Mam was born. Dad is the middle child of three, one brother, Frank, six years older and a sister 13 months younger. His dad died in 1969, which was the year before I was born. Mam comes from a large family of 10 children, there were seven boys and three girls, and Mam is the fourth eldest. Mam's mam, Granny Doug (May) died on 1st October 2001, and her dad Denny died on 3rd December 1986. Mam has lots of nieces and nephews. Granny Doug was great at remembering all of her grandchildren. She remembered all of our birthdays. Right up to the week she died, she came here to our house in Grange Heights to help celebrate my 31st birthday; Generosity came naturally to her.

Even though she lived alone for the last 16 years of her life, she always cooked more food than she would eat herself, just in case she had visitors who needed a meal. My memories of Grandad Denny were just as nice. He was a heavy smoker but never smoked in my presence; I guess he thought I had enough *things going against me without being a passive smoker. He used to come to Crumlin with us regularly throughout my childhood and not smoke until he got out in Carlow and then again at Crumlin Hospital; not bad for a chain smoker. I used to consider the house my grandparents lived in was like a railway station, with people constantly coming and going. Both Granny and Grandad loved people calling, and it was just as well because I sometimes wondered how the front door stayed on its hinges!*

Granny Keever, my great granny, is another person I have happy memories of. She lived in Templeorum, Co. Kilkenny. Her husband, Joe Keever, died on 9th January 1966, so sadly, I never met him. That was the year Mam and Dad married. Mam tells me he was a very jolly man who loved children. I visited Granny Keever very often. In the late '70s, she moved to Waterford to live with Granny Doug and spent the last few years of her life in St Patrick's Hospital, which is down the road from us. She often came up to our house for a few hours, and Dad would wheel me down to visit her in the hospital.

Up to the end of her life, I saw a lot of her. She was into her 93rd year when she slipped away quietly; a wonderful woman.

MY BIRTH AND DISABILITY

I was born on Friday 25th September 1970 in Waterford. An ambulance was called, and I was immediately brought to Our Lady's Hospital in Crumlin, Dublin. I was diagnosed with spina bifida, a defect that is part of the spinal cord and covering. Symptoms include paralysis of the legs, bowel incontinence and urinary incontinence, as well as loss of skin sensation in the legs and an inability to feel hot or cold, which can lead to accidental injury.

My back was operated on the following morning by Professor Eddie Guiney. I was put in an incubator after the operation and remained there for seven weeks. I was checked constantly, and my head was measured daily because when my back was closed, there was a danger of fluid building. Mr Guiney, as he was known then (later to become Professor), said he would err on the side of caution.

At three weeks, a Spitz-Holter valve (a one-way valve system to drain cerebrospinal fluid in order to control hydrocephalus) was inserted into the ventricles of the vein and drained into either the atrium or the peritoneum. Mam and Dad were totally unaware that there was anything wrong with me until I was born. But as soon as I arrived, it was very obvious.

Before I left in the ambulance, there was another big problem. I did not have a name! Dad stepped in and called me 'Ingrid', which means 'hero's daughter.' So, I got the name Ingrid and was baptised before I left for Crumlin. After my surgery on the closing of my back, Mr Guiney spoke to my parents; his exact words were as follows.

"There are mild, moderate and severe degrees of spina bifida. Your daughter has such a severe degree of spina bifida that the likelihood of her surviving is not good."

Professor Guiney

On the occasions that I have heard Mam relive that point of my life story, my reaction has always been that "Someone forgot to tell me that I was not supposed to live."

My pregnancy with Ingrid was straightforward. We already had Graham, who was three years old and had been born just over a year after Ernie and I got married. Ernie and I had no clue whatsoever that there was anything wrong during my second pregnancy. It ended up being a forceps delivery and Ingrid weighed in at a very healthy 9lb. Ernie and I had never even heard of Spina Bifida. I remember as soon as Ingrid was born, they wrapped her in a blanket and whisked her away in an ambulance. I didn't see the awful state her back was in, but I did see her perfect little face peeping out of the blanket.

Just as they were taking her to Crumlin Hospital, Ernie decided we should name her Ingrid. One single name for one unique, brave little girl. They drove off, and I was left behind wondering what on earth was wrong with our precious girl. She was 10 days old before I was well enough to go and see her, and I will never forget seeing her for the first time. She was not a pretty sight! Her back was bumpy, rough and terribly misshapen, and she had horrendous ugly bruising to her head from the forceps delivery. My honest first thought was, "Is she really ours?"

On that first day we met Ingrid, Ernie took Graham to the zoo to give me time alone to feed and bond with her. I held her close, and from the word go, she was a brilliant feeder. At some stage during those first days, I recall Ernie and I sitting across a huge mahogany table from the consultant as he fiddled with his pen and told us Ingrid was from the category within spina bifida that didn't exist yet because no one who had the condition that badly had ever survived before.

Already our little Ingrid was defying the odds. She had begun as she meant to go on; with sheer determination.

We were given leaflets about spina bifida, and I also remember looking it up in the dictionary. There was no Google in those days! I didn't have a clue what we were dealing with nor what was ahead of us.

Looking at Ernie in despair as we drove home with Ingrid in the car, I asked him how on earth we were going to cope. His reply is forever etched on my mind.

"Mary, we will love her as much as we can for as long as we can."

And that is exactly what we did for almost 49 miraculous years.

Being back home with baby Ingrid was terrifying. We constantly checked on her and to say the first six weeks were difficult is undoubtedly an understatement. However, when we took her back to Crumlin, they were completely blown away by her progress. She was happy and thriving.

Then, at only 20 months old, I took her to Lourdes. She was charming the birds out of the trees by that stage with her beautiful blonde curly hair and huge constant smile. I came back from that trip so grateful that Ingrid was as good as she was. So many children were much, much worse. I took her to Lourdes several times over the years, and she went a few times without me.

In 1972 when Ingrid was just two years old, Ernie and I became co-founders of a local Spina Bifida Association. This blossomed into a very loyal, honest and supportive group. We met every month and invited various professional speakers to give talks to parents. Professor Guiney, Ingrid's surgeon, was one of these. A physio also visited the group every Saturday. The parents attending the group became a lifeline for each other and built very close relationships, as did their children. It was particularly difficult for everyone when two of the children, a little boy and a little girl, passed away due to complications related to spina bifida.

Ernie was a tremendously talented carpenter and upholsterer by trade, but his skills went beyond that. He was a wonderful inventor and was passionate about designing bespoke contraptions to make the lives of children living with spina bifida easier and more fun. For the group, he made roly-polies which were basically large cushions/stools that enabled the children to leave their wheelchairs and safely gain access to the floor space together. So effective were Ernie's creations for Ingrid that over the years, hospital professors advised him to patent his products. However, I think for modest, quiet Ernie, the smiles on the children's faces as they used and enjoyed his inventions just as he'd intended was reward enough.

The support group didn't faze out until Ingrid was in her 30s, but Ernie and I weren't involved by then.

Reflecting on those early years, I am very aware that Ernie and I pulled together during a very challenging and upsetting time, when many other couples broke apart. At that time, we knew several couples who ended up getting divorced because they couldn't cope. Taking care of a child with Spina Bifida can be a huge undertaking.

From day one, we did what we could to ensure that Ingrid lived life to the full but to be honest, we didn't need to try very hard. From birth, Ingrid showed a strength of character and courage that I will never see again.

Her physical and emotional strength was unparalleled. Even as a baby striving to reach the milestones of any able-bodied child, she excelled and inspired everyone around her, old and young.

Our life centred around Ingrid, and this life was fun, active and truly blessed. As it turned out, Ingrid ended up streets ahead of both her older and younger brothers developmentally (Gordon was born 11 years after Ingrid). She also talked earlier than both boys and knew all her colours sooner than they did. Ingrid hit all her milestones early, and she even made up for not being able to walk by manoeuvring herself around the floor at speed on her bum, using her hands for leverage. So swift was her movement that I remember her appearing in the front garden one day, although she was only a tiny 10 months old. She had shuffled her way out the front door on her bum, down the steps and over to me. I couldn't believe my eyes when I looked down and there she was in her navy pants and red top looking up at me, as cute as you like!

My early days were spent at Lismore Lawn, a new two-story semi- detached house. From what I am told, days and weeks went by with me being the centre of attention with loving parents, a doting big brother, grandparents and extended family.

I was taken to Dublin for check-ups every few months. I played on the floor with 'Game' (my brother Graham) minding me, I pulled myself about using my arms, and I believe I got in cupboards, pulling all in there out. In 1974, my parents bought a site in Grange Heights in Waterford to enable them to build a bungalow as they were looking to the future. The St John of God primary school was less than a mile from where our new bungalow had been built. Mam approached them. As there was no other child with a disability in any mainstream school, it had to be discussed in detail. I had to be brought to Our Lady's Hospital, Dublin, for a psychological assessment to see if I was capable of mainstream school.

At the end of 1973 and into 1974, I attended St John of God preschool. The nun in charge, Sister Annunciata, was known to us children as Nuncy, and Nuncy she remained. She was and is the most amazing person; she was and is our very own Mother Teresa. At that stage, the preschool in St John of God's had both boys and girls. Dad made a special chair for me, but the boys wanted me to play with them on the floor. Nuncy would put me on a floor rug, and the boys used it as a magic carpet and pulled me from one end of the room to the other. We children thought it was great fun. But poor Nuncy will tell you to this day that her heart was in her mouth praying that no harm would come to me.

When it came time for Ingrid to go to school, we were very keen that she went to mainstream school. I had watched her develop quickly and shuffle her way through all the typical childhood challenges with ease. I had unrelenting faith in our daughter's ability, and I wasn't afraid of sharing this faith with others.

In 1974, Ingrid began attending St John of God Preschool, and she fit in there so very well. All the children loved her, the staff loved her, and she loved them.

Nuncy was the loveliest little person in this world and is still alive in her 90s. Ingrid absolutely adored her, and she, Ingrid. She was so saintly, so motherly and caring. She was like a real-life tiny angel, standing at under five foot tall. I remember coming into the nursery room, and there would be bits and pieces of underwear drying round the room that she'd washed through if the children had an accident. Nuncy was so generous that she even had a nun's habit made specially, with a big pocket to hold all the sweets she would take around the hospital when on her regular visits.

Perhaps Nuncy's most likeable trait was her playfulness and understanding of a child's need to play, interact and take risks. Ingrid was in the special chair that her dad had made for her at this stage, which meant that she was raised up off the floor. The chair was fantastic. It was like a lower version of a baby's high-chair on castors. It didn't impress the boys in the group though, they wanted Ingrid down on the floor with them. So, thinking about what would be best for Ingrid in terms of her emotional and physical development, what did little Nuncy do? Only put Ingrid on the floor!

For hours on end, the boys would pull Ingrid round and round the room on that 'magic carpet'. It was just a small rug to you or me, but a fantastical means of transport for carefree

Ingrid and her friends. I know in my heart of hearts that Nuncy was one of those people in our lives who appreciated, as much as we did, that Spina Bifida placed only a physical limitation on Ingrid and certainly not a mental one. So, she did everything she could to involve Ingrid in stimulating play to ensure she never felt left out or different.

Our wedding, 19th October 1966

Graham's first communion

Granny Doug and Ingrid together for Ingrid's birthday

Ingrid's first trip to Lourdes

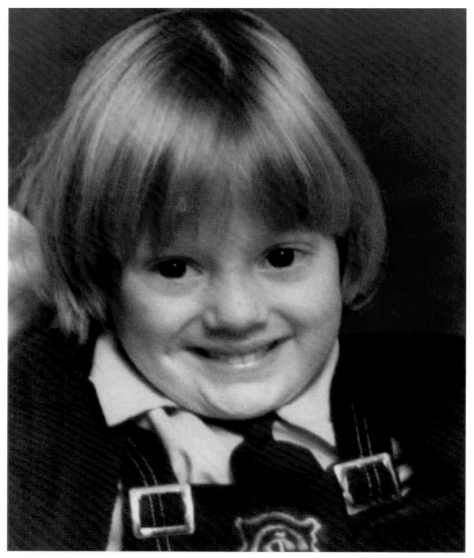

Ingrid's first days at school in her John of God's uniform

3 - HOSPITAL, HEALING, HOME

Around this time (1974), I started having daily headaches and became irritable, which I am told was out of character for me. When I was taken to Crumlin Hospital, I was told the catheter from my shunt (this is the Spitz Holtzer valve) to my heart needed to be lengthened, but this was done successfully. When I was there, the skin on my back had broken, so Mr Regan, the orthopaedic surgeon, decided to reduce the lump on my back. The operation was a major one called a spinal osteotomy. Mam and Dad were told it was a 50/50 chance operation. I was in hospital from 8th March 1974 until 28th June 1974. Mam was with me most of the time; she stayed in the hospital when there was a bed available and in a B&B when there wasn't. I was in ICU for weeks after the surgery, and only Mam and Dad were allowed in to visit.

One day, Dad drove from Waterford alone; when he arrived, he had to don a white coat before being allowed to see me. He entered the room when a lady doctor and a nurse with Mam helping were just about to put up another unit of blood. There was a splash of blood, and Dad fainted. All of us women laughed as he was hauled onto the balcony to be revived. Sure, that's men for you, one sight of blood and they're gone!

The medical profession could not get my back to heal; they said they might have to do a skin graft. On 28th June, Mr Regan spoke with Mam and Dad and asked them if they were prepared to take me home to see if my back would heal. I left Crumlin with them that day. There was great excitement in Waterford as it was my Aunt Lucy's, mam's younger sister's wedding day. Graham was a page boy. After church, my Aunt Hilda and Uncle Michael (my godfather) looked after me until my parents returned from the wedding reception. I had to lie on my tummy the whole time as I could not sit.

The following day, Dad went to the workshop and made a special trolley on big wheels for me. It was like a hospital trolley. He upholstered it and put a tray effect on the front that I used for colouring, playing with plasticine, washing my dolls and, of course, my meals. It also had a shelf underneath for dressings as my back had to be dressed several times a day. I still had to wear a plaster cast for part of the day. I was wheeled about and lifted onto the bed at night. Six weeks later, I was brought back to Mr Regan, and he was amazed. He asked for permission to take photographs of my back to show his medical students. He said to Mam and Dad, "You did at home what we at Our Lady's Hospital failed to do."

Once again, there is no place like home!

At around 3 and a half years of age, my placid, happy- go-lucky Ingrid started behaving out of character. I knew something was badly wrong when one minute she was sitting happily on the settee eating chips and sausage, and the next she had fired the plate across the room. Ingrid's eyes always told me a lot, and when I looked at them that day, they were full of pain and frustration. She also had a high temperature. I went into autopilot, phoned Crumlin and quoted her medical number 100242 down the phone. They told me to put her in the car and bring her in. She was no stranger to hospital, having had a few minor operations before this.

While she was in hospital, her back broke down, and they had no choice but to perform a very risky operation. Although Ingrid's account of events states that the doctors said it was 50/50 whether the operation on her back would be a success, they had actually said it was 60/40, on the wrong side! Once again, the odds were stacked against our girl.

We didn't have any choice. I knew if we didn't at least try this operation, infection would set in, and we would most certainly lose her. It was a terrifying experience, and Ingrid lost so much blood on the operating table.

After the operation, they were finding it impossible to heal Ingrid's back in the hospital and eventually asked if we would be willing to take her home and attempt to heal it there. On the 3-and-a-half-hour journey home in the car, I had to sit very straight on the back seat with Ingrid lying across me, face-down because we couldn't bend her or put any pressure on her back.

That day was particularly stressful because it was my sister Lucy's wedding day, and Graham was meant to be a pageboy. The wedding was at 4 p.m., and at midday, we were still in Crumlin hospital.

Adding even more time pressure was the fact that there was a young girl being dismissed from hospital with a broken leg but had no one to pick her up and take her home to Waterford. So, Ernie and I offered. When we got to her house, there was no one there, which delayed us even further.

Eventually, a neighbour took her in, and we finally headed for home.

We only had time to get Graham ready before making a dash for the church. We brought Ingrid with us to church, and of course, she was the centre of attention, as always. Everyone was so delighted and relieved to see her. She had been in hospital from the 8th March and this was 28th June 1974

At that time, there was a fine film over Ingrid's back which we ensured stayed intact at all times. It was a beautiful balmy summer that year, and I decided to try laying Ingrid at the open window as much as possible with just a bit of gauze on her back and let the warm breeze gently caress her broken skin.

The fresh air worked wonders, when combined with the trolley and when we took her back to Crumlin Hospital, the consultant couldn't believe it. I will never forget him telling us (very graciously) that we managed to do at home what they couldn't do in Crumlin.

As Ingrid mentioned, he was so impressed that he took photos of Ingrid's back to show his students. It felt so wonderful that our home had been such a healing and comforting place for Ingrid.

Graham as pageboy for Lucy's wedding to Kevin Whittle - with Isobel as flower girl

4 - CARS, CHAIRS, COMMUNION

I was always in the middle of whatever was going on when I was little. Dad got me a special red car with joysticks when I was five. He put an upholstered seat in it, so that it was more comfortable and I only needed my hands to drive. It got me about very quickly. I took it to parties with me, so I was never left sitting there. It was a great attraction on the street in our cul-de-sac as my playmates always wanted a go on it.

My first few years in St John of Gods Primary School saw me with Sr. Mary Curran, Miss Rose Mc Geary, Mrs Kenneally, Miss Marie Kennedy and Sr. Mary of the Angels; all of them were very helpful. Sr Mary Curran encouraged me to perform in the Féile in the Theatre Royal with my classmates, something I thought I could never do. As they say, where there's a will, there's a way, and I had a wrought iron will.

As I was prone to kidney infections, I was advised to drink plenty of water, and it was not an easy task. Rose McGeary took on the job of getting water into me. She'd supervise me drinking at break time, and on occasions, she put a senior girl in charge. That girl knew she would be in trouble if I didn't finish the water, so some days the flowers were watered when I refused to drink.

I had lots of friends at school. They often came to our house after school to play with me, and I often visited friends' houses. I had a special friend, Richelle Cahill. Her mam, Joan, often brought me to Glenville to play. Richelle had a younger brother,

Brian, and all three of us had great fun. Richelle's dad worked in the bank, so when he was transferred up the country, she had to leave John of God's, but we stayed in touch, visited each other and remained friends.

I remember Ingrid's red car with the joysticks so well. She was about five when her dad gave it to her. I would watch her repeatedly spin up and down the cul-de-sac at the speed of light. She was loving life and happily let her friends turf her out onto the pavement while they had a go. I would drive into the cul-de-sac, and there was Ingrid, happy as Larry, lying on the pavement and laughing with her friends as they whizzed past in her red car.

At about eight years old, Ingrid went into leg callipers (a device used to support her to help stand) for a while, and her dad made her a special table with a hole in the centre that she could stand up in. It wasn't long until we all realised the callipers were not doing Ingrid any good and they were causing pressure on her back, so she stopped using them.

We had battled hard to get Ingrid into mainstream school, and she was getting on very well, despite missing out on quite a bit during hospital stays. By the time Ingrid was due to move from the third to the fourth class, which was upstairs, the person in charge would not permit Ingrid to be carried upstairs to class, so she suggested Ingrid repeat the third class. We did not consider this necessary. Ingrid had to repeat third class twice (when she should have been in 4th and 5th class) simply because the fourth and fifth class rooms were upstairs. I applied for and was granted a home tuition grant from the department. I had read where a child with special needs attending a mainstream school could qualify and thought it would help Ingrid given the unfortunate situation in school at the time and it did Ernie was doing upholstery work for O'Sullivan's B&B at the time, and its owners had mentioned that the school inspector was in town and would be staying with them. I saw my opportunity, wrote a letter to the Inspector about Ingrid's schooling and gave it to Ernie to hand-deliver to the owner of the guesthouse who promised to provide it to the inspector as soon as he arrived back.

The inspector likely received the letter around 4 or 4.30pm and at 6 p.m. that evening, the doorbell rang, and there was the school inspector wanting to talk about the letter. I brought him in, and he interviewed Ingrid and me right there in our living room. By the end of this short time with us, so impressed was he with Ingrid that he looked me straight in the eye and said, "leave this with me." Before I knew it, the sixth class (as that is what Ingrid should be in given she had to repeat third class twice) was moved downstairs, and the third class was moved upstairs, and that's something that is still in place in the school today – if a student attends who cannot access classes upstairs then the classes will be swapped around to ensure they can still continue progressing. To this day, this is still something that frustrates me, as it was not a particularly complicated solution for what was a relatively simple problem. I felt that only the will or desire was lacking. I never understood why the person in charge couldn't have thought of this herself. It's beyond me! She certainly discovered then, as many people were to discover in the future, that where Ernie and I were concerned, anything that needed to be done for Ingrid was going to be done! This was something Ernie never forgot as anyone standing in the way of his daughter's progression was not thought highly of.

The year of my First Holy Communion, 1978, was a particularly bad year. In March and April, I started having bad headaches and running a high temperature. Everything would settle down only to start up again later.

When I arrived in Our Lady's Hospital, Crumlin, they did a valve tap, which is where they insert a needle into the shunt and withdraw cerebral spinal fluid for analysis. It was discovered that I had a blocked and infected shunt that needed replacing. The old shunt was replaced, but I was still not very well and was going in and out of a coma. I was going off into another world. When I returned, I told those around me I had been in a beautiful garden with lots of colours, ladies with long, vibrant dresses and everything was very bright.

Eventually, Professor Guiney told Mam and Dad that his back was against the wall, and he felt he had no choice but to operate again. This time, he put in a second shunt beside the original one, but he ran this one down to my peritoneum. So, now I had a VA and a VP shunt. They said that infection might get into the shunt system for no apparent reason, but more often following a revision of the shunt. The germs that cause the infection are often very mild, and the body often destroys them, except when there is a foreign body in the system, for example, a shunt. The normal defences of the body cannot penetrate it, and the germs can then grow within the catheter and colonise the shunt. Less often, more vehement organisms cause the infection.

After this revision, it was thought that I would not make it. My parents decided to have me receive my First Holy Communion in the ICU. Mam, Dad and Graham were with me on that memorable day. However, I'm a fighter and wanted to be with my friends on their ('our') Communion Day. I started to make a slow recovery, and I was discharged home (kicked out!) on 20th May. Against all odds, on 22nd May 1978, I was at St Joseph of Benildus Church in Newtown with my class for Communion Day. I wore a lovely long white dress and veil. Looking back on photographs, I looked very angelic. Of course, everyone was delighted to see me.

I recall only too well when Ingrid was very bad in Crumlin and Prof. Guiney telling Ernie and I that he had no remaining options when it came to treating Ingrid. I remember going to the Chapel in Crumlin Hospital and arguing with God. I challenged him and more or less asked him what on earth he was playing at. He spared Ingrid when she was born and we loved her as much as we could. Yet now, when she was so loved as part of a close and caring family, was he seriously going to take her from us? I shouted "well I have no control over what you are going to do but you better give me the grace to accept and the strength to bear if taking her is what you decide! I left the chapel and returned to Ingrid to be told Prof. Guiney had been looking for me. He returned to the ward later to say he felt he needed to give Ingrid one more chance and he intended taking her back to the theatre to add a third shunt and see if that would help to resolve her deteriorating condition.

I cannot express how proud we felt watching Ingrid in her long white dress taking communion with her friends after all she had been through. Our beautiful, brave girl was genuinely adored by so many. I watched as streams of friends gathered around to get their photos taken with her. When his daughter Aoife came to be photographed with Ingrid, I remember Liam (a family friend and local doctor) saying to me, "Isn't it just so unfair, Mary?" I knew he was referring to Ingrid, her disability and her litany of hospital procedures. Despite understanding why he was saying this, inside, I didn't feel angry or frustrated about Ingrid's journey. Looking at Ingrid's delighted face that day, I knew she didn't either. I looked at Liam, smiled and said, "Yes, but look, she's still smiling!"

I suppose what I was saying to Liam that day was, "Yes, it's been hard, but if Ingrid can still smile through it all, then so can we." And this was how Ingrid handled life. She smiled and laughed through the pain and the frustrations. Let's remember her ability to joke about going a few rounds with Mohammed Ali earlier in her journey. Ingrid had a wicked sense of humour, and it carried all of us through.

Ingrid in her red car

Ingrid playing in her car with friends

Ingrid together with Sister Mary

Ingrid in Féile at Theatre Royal

Ingrid's first communion

Ingrid's communion at Crumlin

*Four generations of the family, taken at
Ingrid's first communion*

Ingrid together with Richelle and Brian Cahill

5 - BIRTHS, BROTHER, BISHOPS

I returned to school in September of that year. I tried to make up for what schooling I had missed. In January 1980, I had more shunt problems and another operation. This time, Mr Guiney inserted a new shunt on the left side of my head just behind the ear, similar to the other, and he ran this catheter down to my peritoneum also. I now had three shunts to contend with. But as long as they were doing what they were intended for, I had no problem with them.

In 1981 my little brother Gordon was born; the excitement in our house was unbelievable. After my birth, Mam and Dad went to a Professor of Genetics in Dublin and were advised not to have more children, as the risk of having another child with spina bifida was great. Also, the previous year Mam was having her own problems and ended up in hospital for the removal of her womb. I once again misbehaved. What else would I do? I ended back up in Crumlin with shunt problems. When Mam heard over the phone that my condition was getting worse, she discharged herself from the hospital to be at my side. After another revision, my recovery was slow but sure. Mam forgot about her operation, and by the time my health was good, she was pregnant.

I can remember clearly the day Mam told Graham and me that she was pregnant. We jumped with delight, and I told Graham to go put the kettle on and make Mam a cup of tea. My big brother Graham and I were godparents to Gordon, and we chose his name. I felt it a great privilege, and I watched over him all the time. I was so delighted, and I thanked God that he was so perfect. From the time he was creeping, he used my wheelchair to pull himself up; he was always sitting on my footrest and getting up on my lap for a spin on the wheelchair. Dad had adapted the lock on the front door so that I could open it myself. One day, Gordon, at only 10 months old, had watched me pull the string, did likewise and was making his way out the steps when Mam caught him. We all had to be extra careful after that as he was walking before his first birthday. He was the centre of attention, and he entertained all of us.

On 19th June 1983, I was confirmed at St Josephs and Benildus Church, Newtown. Bishop Michael Russell, who later became a great friend of mine, performed the ceremony. The parish priest was Fr Raymond Liddane, who was also a great friend and very good to me. The church was packed, and I wore a nice cream dress and a mantilla. After church, everyone came back to our house; it was a beautiful day, and the house and garden were full of very happy people.

I was in Kilkenny for a scheduled hysterectomy operation (we had been advised against having more children given some of the issues I had experienced in the years since Ingrid arrived). The day of the operation coincided with a routine check-up in Dublin for Ingrid. From the hospital, I contacted Crumlin hospital to see how the check-up had gone, only to discover Ingrid had had a nasty turn. Nothing would do but to discharge myself and go to be with her. I cancelled the surgery and headed to be by my daughter's side, where I belonged.

I am sure Ingrid would say this turn of events was meant to be because, a few months after, I discovered that I was pregnant, 11 years after giving birth to Ingrid. According to my gynaecologist, it was a miracle; according to Ingrid, it was the best thing ever. The day I told her, she was like a little granny telling Graham, "Go make Mam a cup of tea!" and telling me, "Mam, put your feet up!"

Needless to say, I was quite anxious during this pregnancy and especially towards the end of labour. I remember feeling so relieved when the reassuring voice of my gynaecologist filtered through, "Mary, he's got 10 tiny fingers and 10 tiny toes, and they are all wriggling." He knew how anxious we were given Ingrid's condition.

Of course, we were worried about Spina Bifida, who wouldn't have been in our position. Ingrid and Graham chose the name 'Gordon'. To this day, I don't know how or why they came up with it, but it suits him well. I was keen on naming him Ernie, but his dad didn't want a Big Ernie and Little Ernie in the family.

The first words my beautiful, selfless Ingrid said when Gordon was born, were;

"Mam, isn't it just wonderful that he will be able to walk."

Ingrid absolutely idolised her little brother and was quite happy for him to be the centre of attention.

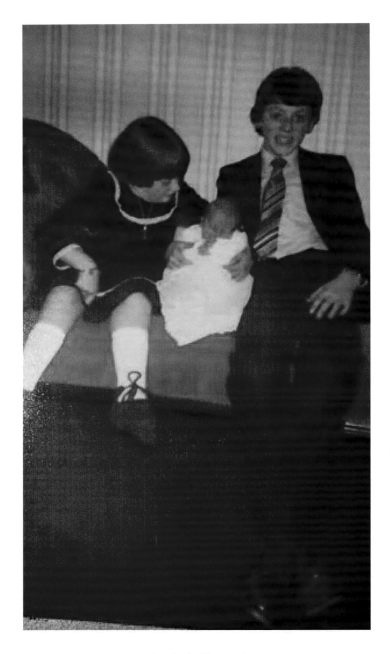

Gordon's Christening

Gordon's first birthday

6 - SCHOOL, COLLEGE, A NEW ADVENTURE

That June (1983) was the end of the primary school years; my friends were starting in various secondary schools in September. Because I had missed so much schooling, my parents felt that I should repeat fifth and sixth class. Mam approached the principal of St Saviour's School, a new wheelchair- friendly school. The principal, Mr Paddy Power, an exceptional man, came to our house to interview me. I started there in September of 1983. The next two years were both enjoyable and eventful. Declan and Máiréad Power, children of the principal, both took me under their wings. It was just as well as it was a very dramatic change for me, and I knew nobody.

The school was a single-storey building and had external doors for each class, which made for very easy access and exit for me. The teachers were both male and female. On my first morning there, Mr Power welcomed me and introduced me to Mr Joe Mc. Laughlin who was the teacher for fifth class. My first morning there went very quickly, and it was the first day that I had ever stayed in school for lunch. Declan and Máiréad stayed with me, and after lunch, they took me on a guided tour of the school. That first year was a novelty, but my second year was really hard work. My sixth-class teacher was Mr O'Sullivan. He gave lots of homework, but the nice thing was that on your birthday you got no homework.

At the end of sixth class, we had an entrance exam for secondary school, and Mr O'Sullivan gave me great help and encouragement. It certainly paid off; he was also trying to prepare me for secondary school. In my sixth year, I also went on a farm outing to Kildalton College in Piltown with the class. It was great fun, and I very much enjoyed it.

In 1983, I visited Lourdes with CASA, that's the Caring and Sharing Association; caring and sharing is what they do, and do well at that. It was more like a holiday than a pilgrimage, and I loved it. This was not my first trip to Lourdes; I had been there many times. Mam took me there when I was only 20 months old, but this was the first time without my parents, so I felt very grown-up.

In 1985, I started at St Paul's College. They were in the planning stage of building the college when we lived in Lismore Lawn, and Mam saw the plans had no ramps or wheelchair facilities. She approached the Parish Priest, who lived a few doors from us. He saw to it that the plans were put right, and I was the first of many pupils in a wheelchair to start there.

It was a very different experience, but thanks to St Saviour's, I had become used to the mixed classes. Nevertheless, the number of students coming and going was mind-boggling, and it took some adjusting to. The first thing I had to get used to was the number of teachers and subjects. Some teachers I got on well with and others not so well, but overall, I coped. I said to myself, "my classmates are coping, so if they are, why can't I?" Some teachers challenged me without fear; they went out of their way not to treat me differently from any other student, and I admired them for that. Some teachers expected a lot from me, and others *let me get away with little work. I realise now the ones who worked me were doing it for my own good. My favourite subjects were art and drama taught by Mr Pat O'Brien, home economics taught by Ms Eileen Power, and English, which I am good at. When I could manage the maths, I enjoyed it, but that wasn't always the case. History was OK, but Geography, I hated it with a passion!*

During my second year in St Paul's, Mr O'Brien decided we were going to perform a play. He wanted me to perform the main part. I had been out of school due to my Grandad Doug's death. I felt very sad as I was very close to him. I was in no mood for plays on my return to school. I said to Mr O'Brien that it would be too difficult to get me on the stage and his response was that we would cross that bridge when we came to it. He was so right, as practising for that play took my mind off thinking of Grandad all the time. After that, I never argued with Mr O'Brien as he knew best. He encouraged me to broaden my artistic horizons, and I am so grateful to him for that. During my time at St Paul's, I had some very good friends and some very happy times.

We were so proud of all of Ingrid's achievements in and out of school. She excelled at art. She loved to cook, perform and succeed. She worked hard to get to the next stage of her school life. Her teachers were brilliant with her, and many went the extra mile to ensure she discovered and channelled new talents.

When Mr O'Brien encouraged Ingrid to take part in the play despite her grandfather having just passed away, I was delighted. I really admired him for that because it did Ingrid a world of good. She loved her Grandad Doug dearly. They had many laughs together. I remember one time he was at our house and sitting in a rocking chair. He liked a little whiskey now and again, and on this day, he was happily clutching a dram after finishing a glass of red wine when somehow the chair toppled, and he toppled with it!

There he was, with his legs in the air, and there was Ingrid just behind him laughing her head off for all the world to hear. Ingrid loved a good laugh, and so did her Grandad Doug.

I think of the fun and the freedom Ingrid had in her big customised trolley and then the red car that her dad adapted for her. It stands in stark contrast in my mind to the memory of the dreadful day Ingrid got her first wheelchair when she was nine and a half years old.

Ingrid was not a fan of wheelchairs! How on earth could she 'stand out' in a wheelchair? She was well aware that many people saw wheelchairs as the intrusive, bulky seats on wheels for those invisible, disabled people of society! Where Ingrid was concerned, a wheelchair risked engulfing the person sitting in it! A wheelchair was in danger of swallowing up its user's personality.

If Ingrid had to be in one of them, she would make it her mission to be an inspiration to all wheelchair users. Ingrid knew a wheelchair would only cast a shadow over the user if they let it. And no wheelchair was ever going to usurp Ingrid. She was a 'hero's daughter', a real-life heroine.

I will not lie; it was still a very traumatic day for all of us when Ingrid sat in a wheelchair for the first time. I think it hit us that this was life for Ingrid from now on and there was a sadness about it. But from the word go, Ingrid made sure people saw her smile, personality, energy and talents long before they saw the chair.

Despite her relentless, soft-hearted way with others, Ingrid's confidence in who she was and what she stood for never weakened. This strength was fully on display in 1987 when Ingrid was 17, and a new wheelchair arrived for her. She had been waiting months and months for her latest aid to arrive. However, much to her horror, when it did, it was turquoise!

She was nothing short of offended by this. In front of the Occupational Therapist who had brought it, Ingrid despaired, "Mam, I never asked for a turquoise wheelchair! If I had wanted turquoise, I would have asked for it!"

And then she declared, *"I don't want people to see the chair before they see me. I don't want a brightly coloured chair. I will bring the colour!"*

Almost as soon as the words came out of Ingrid's mouth, she panicked.

"Oh, Mam, I hope I didn't sound rude. I don't mean to be rude. I just don't want a turquoise wheelchair, and I'm not going to sit in it."

I don't know whether the woman thought Ingrid was rude or not, but I certainly didn't, and I reassured her.

"You're not rude, Ingrid. I am so proud of you that you know what you want to sit in. I'm delighted that you have the courage and the words to be able to stick up for yourself and say so. There are many people out there who would just go ahead and

take the chair and be unhappy in it. *You know your own mind, and that is fantastic."*

Needless to say, Ingrid sent that chair back and got a plain black one in its place which I had to give an undertaking to pay £225 of a difference for before it was ordered.

At Easter 1987, I had another chance to visit Lourdes, this time with the IHCPT, the Irish Handicap Children's Pilgrimage Trust. We each had our own carer; mine was Karen Kelly. As Karen was a teacher in St Saviour's School, I already knew her as Miss Kelly, but Karen wasn't long putting a stop to that, and she became Karen. During the plane journey, Fr Stephen O'Brien started talking to me. He asked if I was attending school. After telling him that I was at St Paul's College, he asked me if I knew Mr O'Brien. I said, of course, and started to give out about Mr O'Brien insisting on my playing a part in the school drama just after my Grandad had died. When I had finished giving out, Fr O'Brien nicely informed me that they were brothers; once again, I had put my foot in it big time!!

During that time, I was going through a lot of uncertainty about my life. I had already finished my second year at St Paul's and was very unsure of my capabilities of further education. We had a great time in Lourdes, and at the end of the week, I had my mind made up to do my Group Cert (nowadays we know it as the Junior Cert!) The year was very tough. I was under pressure and had a lot of work to do, as I had taken it easy for the previous two years. In 1988, I sat the Group Cert; once the exams started, nervous as I was, I got on with it. The art was divided into two parts, imaginative composition in the morning and still life in the afternoon. Imaginative composition involves using your imagination to draw a picture. This was not as easy a task as it sounds, but I enjoyed it. The still life I had reservations about; I was sitting outside the exam room waiting to go in when Mr O'Brien arrived and suggested I break a leg. There is nothing quite like laughter to relax one, and it certainly worked. Home economics was easy enough. My teacher was extremely encouraging, and she helped me through the year. Then maths, my worst nightmare, went better than I expected as I ended up getting a C honour. And English, which of course, I loved, and I also received a C honour for that.

On the day of the results, Mr Russell, the school principal phoned me and asked me if I would return and do another year of St Paul's, which was guaranteed to be totally different. They were starting a new project, a work preparation course, and I decided I would give it a try. It meant four days in college each week, and every Friday was a day doing work preparation. That year I learned to type, which was difficult for me with my left hand because since one of my first shunt operations I had a weakness in it. The teacher insisted that I did my best, and I did.

When it came to work experience, I did some of mine at Rehab, a National Learning Network (NLN) in an industrial estate in Waterford. Rehab provides a range of free courses to people who have had an accident, illness, injury, disability or extra support needs. I did some work for the general industrial part of the factory, which entailed the packing of small parts of games for Milton Bradley. This was a very tedious task, and I didn't like it, but it had to be done. What I did enjoy very much was the office part: answering phones, taking messages and filing. One thing I missed that year was the art and drama, but we did have some home economics classes that I loved.

After that year, I did a year of secretarial and bookkeeping at the Central Technical Institute in Parnell Street. I did not like bookkeeping, and I was very slow at typing, but still, I managed. Eventually, I did two years at Rehab, a National Learning Network (NLN) in the industrial estate in Waterford. It was here I began to write my life story in earnest. Evelyn Waters, one of the tutors, encouraged me. I already had a few bits and pieces done in copybooks, and I started to format it and get it into some kind of order. I probably would have stuck with my story then, but for another diversion, a Computer Foundation Course at the Waterford Institute of Technology. Evelyn encouraged me to apply for a place, and I was accepted. I spent a year at WIT and loved it and received a cert.

I also did some work experience at the National Rehabilitation Board in Gladstone Street in Waterford.

After that, as I enjoyed computers, I did a two-year course from home where a tutor came to my house every week. I had a certain number of assignments and study days, and I thoroughly enjoyed it and got my computer cert at the end of the two years.

Receiving her Computer Foundation Course certificate was one of the highlights of Ingrid's life, and I have the pictures to prove it. My brother Kevin, Ingrid's uncle, wrote this poem at that time to express just how proud the whole family was of her:

A DREAM REALISED

She held it aloft,
Rolled high like a baton.
The Instamatics flashed.
Her parents shunned the limelight,
As she held court with the media.
Seated in her own personal chariot
Slouched slightly forward,
Her glistening blue eyes
Barely visible through her blond hair
Cascading down her face.
Easing my way across the room
I crouched down as if in adoration.
She held my hand and exclaimed
"I did it. I really did it!"

By Kevin Douglas, Uncle

In the 80s we had an electric typewriter in our home, followed by a word processor. I used these to do Ernie's business accounts and administration. Eventually we got Ingrid a computer to encourage her to use her hands. As she has mentioned, Ingrid had a weakness in her left hand ever since an early shunt procedure (at about the age of seven). I used to put her charm bracelet, which her dad gave her for her first birthday, on her left hand to encourage her to use it because she loved the sound it made. We got her a CD called 'Mavis Beacon Teaches Typing' in the 1990s and Ingrid taught herself to type. Gordon also learned to type on his sister's computer with Mavis Beacon and Ingrid's support. To this day he is eternally grateful as it stood him in great stead at college, when he had to write essays that were thousands of words. Ingrid loved working on the computer and became very proficient over the years.

She taught me everything I know about computers, and I am so grateful for that. She showed me how to connect to the internet (it was a dial-up modem back then!) and to access and send emails to Graham in Japan. We both loved to play solitaire on the computer as well, and I would often play it when I was at my most anxious about her.

Taking up the story again, Ingrid explains that after she completed her computer cert in 1992:

I attended the Adult Education Centre for art and also for creative writing. I had the same Mr Pat O'Brien teaching me art for one of the years, and I had Mr Kieran Lynch teaching me for the remaining years. Mark Roper was the teacher in charge of the creative writing class. I very much enjoyed my time there and learned a lot.

The highlight of my year every year from 1985 until 2003 was Share Music. Share Music was held in the Share Centre in Lisnaskea, Co. Fermanagh. It was a musical talent week for people with various disabilities and bundles of ability. They travelled from all over the world for a week of hard work, plenty of great fun and a heavenly result.

Behind this great event every year was Dr Michael Swallow, a neurologist and his team. He started this from nothing and went on to be awarded an OBE by Queen Elizabeth for his marvellous work. He and his wife, Barbara, took a personal interest in all our endeavours. Professional tutors were brought in to organise us and help us. On the first morning, we were introduced to a project, which we worked on daily. Each course had a different emphasis, but all worked towards a final performance given to an invited audience at the end of the week. The atmosphere was electric, and everything came together so well. We even performed in the Waterfront in Belfast.

Every year Michael Swallow brought in a professional tutor. One year we had Richard Stilgoe, a British songwriter, musician and broadcaster. He wrote to me after his trip back home telling me to keep going, I was doing well. He's another who was awarded an OBE from Queen Elizabeth for his charitable work in working with people with disabilities.

In 1998, 2000 and 2002, Share Music came to the Cuisle Centre in Roscommon, a beautiful holiday centre for people with disabilities, which was taken over by The Wheelchair

Association, on the grounds of Donamon Castle – one of the oldest inhabited buildings in Ireland. One year, when we were doing 'A Midsummer Night's Dream' in the beautiful chapel with amazing acoustics, I was crossing the stage.

Dad and Mam were seated on the altar. Dad shifted his seat to get a better look, and low and behold, didn't it come off the step making a very loud bang! Poor Dad. Later, when Dr Michael Swallow was giving his talk, he said jokingly, "First, I would like to ask Mr Walsh not to be trying to upstage his daughter." Dad, a very reserved man, was totally mortified.

These were very exciting years, the journey every year was very long, but I looked forward to it. My parents drove me up on a Saturday and returned the following week for the Grand Finale show before I said goodbye for another year. I attended this event every year, with the exception of 1993 when I was packed and ready to go, but I ended up in Beaumont Hospital. It was so lovely to discover that I was missed and thought of when Dr Swallow kindly phoned our home to check on me.

As I was pulling together all of the content for this book, I asked many people for input, stories and memories to try and include. Two of Ingrid's cousins (Fiona, who now lives in Australia, and Sabrina, who is in Waterford) were recently reminiscing and Fiona recalled attending Share Music one year in Enniskillen with Ingrid. Her abiding memory was of Ingrid keeping her up all night to listen to music and her attempts to manage the exhaustion the following day!

Fiona also recalled how Ingrid's wheelchair made all her friends and family much more aware of the challenges presented to people using one. Whenever she was younger and Ingrid was spending an afternoon or a day at her house, her father (Michael, my brother) would have to take the screen off the front porch so that Ingrid and her wheelchair could get through the door. She remembers Ingrid always being so apologetic at causing such an inconvenience. Thankfully our awareness (and building regulations) has moved on dramatically since then.

In June 1993, when I was 23, I was to have another shunt revision this time. I was in theatre, and when the surgeon removed the catheter to my peritoneum, he perforated my bowel. They then had to get a general surgeon to repair my bowel. They decided not to go ahead with the revision, as opening my head just then didn't seem a good idea for fear of cross-infection. I was allowed home to recover even though I was still to have that shunt replacement.

Ernie and I relished going to see Ingrid performing in any arts or music shows she was involved in. As for Mr O'Brien, she was supposedly so cross with him for making her do the play; it was as clear as day to everyone that Ingrid adored him, and I'm so glad that she thanks him in her own writing for cajoling her onto the stage. I will never forget when Ingrid moved on to the Adult Education Centre, and Mr O'Brien was her art teacher. She announced to us, "Oh Mam, we aren't at school anymore. It's Pat now. Just plain Pat. None of this formal Mr O'Brien anymore."

Ingrid was at home on the stage. She blossomed in front of an audience.

We always knew that Share Music had a very special place in her heart, as it did ours. Every year we made the four-and-a-half-hour journey to Lisnaskea and left her in the capable hands of the wonderful Michael Swallow and his team. Ernie and I then went and stayed with friends in Ballyshannon, Co Donegal. We were able to fully relax knowing that Ingrid had a wonderful one-to-one carer at Share Music, Nurse Elizabeth. When we wondered what she might be up to, we knew it was anyone's guess. Our feisty, energetic little girl could be sailing on a river, wall-climbing (really! I've included the photo on page 84) or singing her little heart out on the stage for all we knew. There was no activity that Ingrid would shirk.

In the mid-'90s, Phil Coulter was due to play at the Theatre Royal. I was a huge fan and desperate to go, but there were no tickets left except for disabled guests and their helpers. Well, that was it... I was going, and Ingrid was going to have to come with me! The slight problem was that Ingrid didn't want to go. She had no interest in Phil Coulter or his music. He was no Michael Jackson or Bob Geldof, after all! I jokingly told Ingrid that if she didn't come with me, I would have to borrow her wheelchair, and her Dad would have to wheel me in.

Eventually, Ingrid gave in and went with me and was extremely glad she did. Phil Coulter's support act was the Irish Tenors and after the show that night, they chatted to Ingrid for ages. Ingrid was clearly delighted and forever afterwards loved Phil Coulter's music. A few years later, when Phil Coulter was playing in the The Forum, it didn't take much persuasion to get Ingrid to go. The Irish tenors, who were now calling themselves The Celtic Tenors, were supporting once again, and after the show, they and Phil Coulter came over to sign autographs and speak to Ingrid. They remembered her name and the conversation they'd had with her the last time. I often think Phil Coulter had a special affinity with the likes of Ingrid because he was the father of a child with special needs who died.

Ingrid lit up lives everywhere she went. Such was her infectious smile and genuine empathy that meeting Ingrid was not something anyone could forget in a hurry. From random customers in her favourite bookstore to renowned musicians, once they had encountered Ingrid, that experience was stored and cherished in their memory bank forever.

And Ingrid treated everyone exactly the same. She didn't want to be treated differently because of her wheelchair and she applied those same rules to everyone else she encountered too.

Meeting, greeting and later, public motivational speaking was becoming one of Ingrid's most prominent talents and regular pastimes.

Ingrid climbing the wall at Share Music

Ingrid in procession at Share Music

Ingrid and Lucy on the night Ingrid received her computer cert

Pat O'Brien, Ingrid's beloved art teacher

Ingrid receiving the award from the principal of St Paul's College, Tony Russell, on his retirement

7 - BEST FRIENDS, BRIDESMAIDS, SETBACKS

Life continued to have its ups and downs for our family and Ingrid's health.

A significant high was Ingrid's 21st birthday and our 25th wedding anniversary in 1991 when we had a special mass at home. Fr Liddane celebrated it, and although we already knew, we only had to look around at all the people gathered to see just how popular Ingrid had become. Her beloved Sr Nuncy and Sr Una attended and Sr Una even brought along her organ and some members of her girls' choir who lived in the area to play music and enhance the occasion further.

Then in 1992, our family was dealt a difficult blow, as Ingrid explains...

On 18th May 1992, my Aunty Ann died, and three months later, her daughter Isobel married Aidan Power. It was a sad and happy day, but I am sure my Aunty Ann was looking down on them. I was asked to be one of Isobel's bridesmaids, and I was delighted. Thank God for Granny Doug as she took the place of Aunty Ann. It must have been difficult for her as it was for all of them there. But it was a lovely day; everyone rallied around and made the most of it for the bride and groom.

I have a photograph of Ingrid in her beautiful green bridesmaid dress [included on page 97], dancing with the groom, no less, on Isobel and Aidan's wedding day. Like all the pictures I have of Ingrid, I treasure this one. Ingrid was so happy on that day. Isobel was not only her cousin but her best friend, and to be her bridesmaid was a dream come true for Ingrid.

Ingrid's friendship circle and her reputation as an ambassador for people with disabilities were expanding at the rate of knots. By the time she was in her 30s, she counted bishops among her friends and was on the guest list for the inauguration of a new bishop.

Ingrid was such a vibrant, charismatic young woman that all kinds of people radiated to her including people in positions of authority. Ingrid befriended Bishop Russell during the course of her trips to Lourdes, the first of which was in 1972. I can't even recall exactly how her friendship started with Bishop Michael. He just always came to chat to her at mass and I remember he had a housekeeper who I would sometimes give a lift to, as she did not drive herself. She adored Ingrid and would give her chocolate, which Ingrid loved. Bishop William Lee encountered Ingrid when he visited REHAB where she worked. Ingrid loved to meet and greet at events and was always chosen to do so because of her natural way with people. From his first encounter Bishop William Lee became very fond of her and any event they were both attending he would have made a point of speaking to her.

As a family, we geared up for Bishop Lee's inauguration for quite some time; however, as anticipation mounted, Ingrid's health sadly deteriorated.

In July 1993, I was asked to represent the Wheelchair Association at the inauguration of our new bishop, William Lee. Bishop Michael Russell, my good friend, had retired a few months earlier. I was asked to take part in the offertory procession. It was a great honour, and I looked forward to it. I was still recovering from the June surgery and was not sure whether or not I would be well enough for the Bishop's day. My headaches were bad, and no one could predict how long they would last.

On the day of Bishop William Lee's inauguration, I wasn't well at all. Mam gave me painkillers and kept me resting until the last minute. She knew how much I wanted to be in the Cathedral. She went and got herself dressed whilst I was resting. She wore the outfit that she had worn for Isobel's wedding the previous August. She later got me into the green satin dress that I wore as a bridesmaid.

Mam was under such pressure to get me to the Cathedral that she forgot to pull up her tights. Mam was about to bring me in the offertory procession up the centre when she bent over the wheelchair and said to me, "Ingrid, pray to Aunty Ann and anyone else up there that will listen that my tights will stay where they are and not fall around my ankles!" It would've been so funny if the occasion wasn't so serious. However, Mam lived to tell the tale, and the tights stayed up, thank God!

In August, I had to return to Beaumont, and this time they did the shunt revision, and it was successful.

The fact that Ingrid was asked to attend the Bishop's inauguration is a testament to how popular she was and how people craved her company. This popularity spawned numerous true and lasting friendships. Ingrid didn't make acquaintances; she did true friendship. I cannot tell you how many times someone in a prominent position of authority in the church, world of medicine or politics turned to me and insisted, "Ingrid does more for me than I could ever do for her."

Ingrid was a born listener. She had empathy pouring through her veins. She didn't want to talk to other people about her woes; she wanted to talk through and help with their woes. She didn't want sympathy or pity. She wanted the conversation, stimulation and mutual understanding that only genuine friendships can bring. She almost always responded to the question 'how are you?' by saying something like 'I'm grand' and then quickly followed that up with a question of her own: 'but more importantly, how are you?'.

The way she tells the tights story on the day of the inauguration is typical of how Ingrid could transform a challenging situation into a light-hearted and entertaining one. Ingrid was so very unwell that day, which was why we were running so late. I waited until the very last minute before deciding she was strong enough to attend because I feared she really wasn't but I knew how important the invitation and event were to her.

Looking back on that day, I'm glad it's the funny tights story that Ingrid recalls above everything else, not the pain she was in, the anxiety we were all feeling, or the looming operation scheduled for the following month, which, much to everyone's relief, was successful.

But equally, she knew when to switch the sarcasm and banter off, get serious and empathise fully with anyone who was hurting.

Ingrid's 21st with Father Liddane, Sister Nancy and Una

Ingrid dancing at her 21st

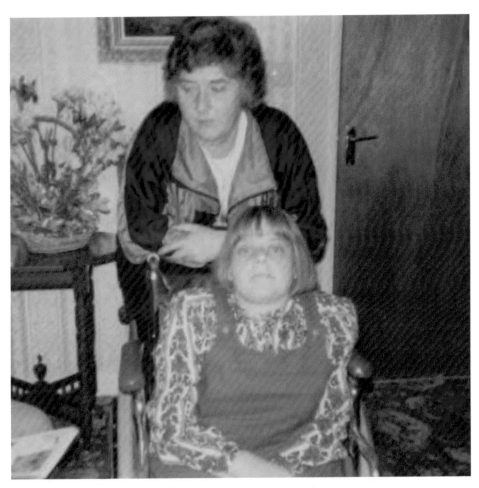

Aunty Ann and Ingrid together

Ingrid as bridesmaid for Aidan and Isobel 1992

8 - TALKS, THOUGHTS, THANKS

After I finished my school years, I was asked to talk to the students in various secondary schools about my disability, coping with it and the reaction of others to the same. I

always found these talks great, and the atmosphere was brilliant. The question-and-answer sessions which followed my talks were always very direct, and the feedback was great. We covered a lot of topics. I was encouraged to visit again and again, and I actually got paid for talking. The number of letters and cards thanking me was overwhelming. It was absolutely great to see how thankful the students were, and so many of them said to me that I gave them food for thought.

The other event I always looked forward to was acting as a polling clerk on election days. There was always a great buzz and plenty of activity, even if they were long days, and I always knew so many people coming in to vote. I even did my training in the Court House on the never-to-be-used E-voting machines that are stored at a huge cost to the poor taxpayers.

These e-voting machines which were bought by the Irish Government in 2002 to be used for all elections were never used. By 2010 they were being sold for scrap. The machines that had cost €51 million in 2002 were sold for €70,000 for the entire lot in the end.

I never attended Ingrid's school talks because I didn't want to put her off in any way. But I know she was amazing because of all the letters she received after them.

This is just one such letter:

"My name is Anne-Marie Byrne, and I am currently sitting my Junior Certificate at Presentation Secondary School. I am currently writing up my Civic Social Political education project and I want to thank you. If it weren't for your help telling us about your disability, I wouldn't be able to do my action project. You taught my classmates and me the meaning of spina bifida and that there is more to people in wheelchairs or with other disabilities than what meets the eye.

My classmates and I are truly grateful for all the help and support you gave us when you came to our school. You took time out of your life to come and talk to us, and we want to thank you so much for helping us with our project. My classmates and I hope you are keeping well and we hope to see you in the future.

I will write to you when I get my results and tell you what I got in my GSPE, and I know I will pass all thanks to you. Thank you so much for helping with our project on spina bifida. You don't know how much it means to us. Thank you for everything.

It would be nice to hear from you again.

Yours gratefully,

Anne-Marie Byrne"

Ingrid did hand-outs and everything for her talks. Friends of the family who had asked her to give the talks and teachers told me afterwards that she had a unique ability to get the students' attention in a way that they had never managed in their long careers. They insisted that Ingrid's audiences would hang on her every word, and she would have them eating out of her hand. The blonde curly-haired smiling baby at Lourdes that people gravitated towards was now an articulate young speaker who people couldn't resist listening to.

I remember one day we were in Ingrid's favourite book shop, Porters in City Square. We always had tea and cake upstairs in the Kylemore Cafe. When we were drinking tea, a group of young people came into the cafe. One fella came over and was so gentle and gracious in his manner. He said to Ingrid, "You came and gave a talk at our school. You were amazing. Because of you, we will never look at someone in a wheelchair in the same way again!"

Although she wasn't one for attention or fame, Ingrid did make her very own TV debut in 1997, when she appeared on **Nationwide** to talk about Spina Bifida and the importance of Folic Acid.

We received so many letters after that programme, praising her and congratulating her on how well she spoke. The first one was from Prof. Guiney saying how proud he was of her. Many of these were from doctors. She was already receiving a Christmas card from her friend Bishop Michael Russell every year. On one occasion, when he saw her on the RTE news receiving a special electric-powered wheelchair from the Girl Guides, he wrote to her saying, "You looked magnificent on the television, Ingrid! Now would you ever mind the 30-mph speed limit." Ingrid was never happy about the powered chair, she preferred to wheel herself. I'm not sure if this was her independent streak or stubbornness but that powered chair was donated to a good cause After the Nationwide programme aired, many others wrote to her, including Mary T O'Brien from Tipperary, one of Ingrid's best friend's aunts. She stated, "When I went shopping, the conversation was about the lovely girl from Waterford that spoke so well on the TV. I was delighted to say you were a special friend of the family for 23 years."

Ingrid was the talk of the town, and Ernie and I were so very proud of her.

We had 10 wonderful years when Ingrid was not in hospital at all. When she wasn't giving inspirational talks to students or adding another string to her bow, she was a doting cousin to Alex and a regular visitor at Granny Doug's, as she recalls here.

On 16th September 2000, my cousin Isobel gave birth to a baby boy, Alex. Isobel visited Granny Doug every Thursday with Alex at her home in Gracedieu Road, and I joined them there also. It was always great fun there. By the time Alex had a baby sister, Anna, in January 2004, sadly, Granny Doug had died three years before that. It was Grange Heights they came to from thereon.

I was the first one called when my mother died. After my mother (Granny Doug) died, I phoned Ingrid to tell her Granny had just died at 3pm. When I came home around 5.30pm Ingrid had taken the phone book and gone through all the numbers of people she felt should be notified and had broken the news to them before I returned home.

Once again, my level-headed daughter performed with such efficiency, using her initiative and applying that natural ability she had to be hands-on and helpful. It transpired that Ingrid had contacted people that I would never have thought of contacting who came to the funeral. People that were important to Granny Doug, people that should have been there.

Bishop Michael Russell - a great friend of Ingrid's, who said a special Mass for her in 2006

Being presented with an electric wheelchair by the Girl Guides

9 - SYSTEMS, SEIZURES, SUFFERING

It had been great not to have to go for hospital check- ups all the time, but little did we know just how difficult the process would be when she did need to go back into the system.

In 2002, when Ingrid began to feel very unwell, we literally couldn't get her transferred to Beaumont Hospital when we desperately needed to.

It was so hard to get back in the system. Gone were the days when I would ring up and quote Ingrid's number, and they would say, "put her in the car and bring her in." There was simply no personal contact at the end of the phone anymore. We had been used to staff knowing us, knowing the family and knowing Ingrid. It made such a difference when you could put a face on who you were talking to and they could put a face and name on you. Now the new automated system of press 1… 2… and 3 etc meant never getting a human at the end of the line.

No one was actually there to know or care who you were talking about. It felt like Ingrid had just become a number.

In 2002 and early 2003, I was not well, but no one knew what was wrong with me. On 23rd July 2003 at 6 p.m. I had a seizure, what the medical profession calls a full-blown tonic clonic seizure. I only remember what Mam told me later when I came around in the hospital. She said I had been out of sorts all day and cranky, and she rang 999 when I had the seizure, and I was admitted to Waterford Regional Hospital. They discovered that I had a urinary tract infection, so they treated me, and I was discharged home.

I continued to be unwell, and in February 2004, I had another full-blown seizure.

This time, they said I had a sore throat, treated me with antibiotics and discharged me home. On 23rd August 2004, I was admitted for the third time to Waterford Regional Hospital for a further seizure. According to the records, it was a full-blown tonic clonic seizure again. Waterford Regional Hospital started me on anti-epileptic drugs. At this stage, WRH felt I should have a neurological review, but no referral was ever made to Beaumont. Mam was very anxious to get me to Beaumont, so she asked spina bifida support worker Collette Darcy to assist, as she felt a letter from the association would help, and it did. On 11th November 2004, I went to see Mr Young in Beaumont; I hadn't seen him since 1993. Mr Young felt that if I had another seizure, I should be sent from Waterford Regional Hospital immediately to Beaumont. I was back to Beaumont for a review at Mr Young's clinic in February 2005.

Mr Young wasn't at the clinic that day, but his registrar, Mr Kelleher, was. I was deteriorating both mentally and physically. I had no energy, chronic daily headaches, intolerance to cold, and had developed gastric problems with abdominal pain and diarrhoea. Mr Kelleher arranged for blood tests to be carried *out. He decided I should see a neurologist and referred me to Mr Norman Delanty at Beaumont. He also referred me back to Waterford Regional Hospital to a gastroenterologist for an investigation of my abdominal pain. I went in as a day patient to Waterford Regional Hospital for a colonoscopy, which was technically unsatisfactory. The doctor then asked the consultant radiologist to do an instant barium enema, which was carried out on 26th April 2005 and was inconclusive. Mam went with me to the X-ray room.*

As I sat outside waiting for Ingrid to be seen, a senior radiologist arrived. He went in only to come straight out again and leave. So, there was no way he was in there during Ingrid's test. It seemed to me that some consultants could do what they liked when they liked! Later when I saw Ingrid's notes, they said her results were 'inconclusive.' I remember thinking to myself, well it's little wonder because there wasn't even a consultant present at her test.

I was also sent to a rheumatologist several times, and he said that there was active inflammation going on somewhere. I was back at Beaumont on 12th May 2005 for another review; this time, I was seen by a Mr Card, CPR in neurosurgery. He said that the bloods taken at the previous appointment in February showed that I had hypochromic microcytic anaemia. Mr Card consulted his Gastroenterology colleagues, who thought I was suffering from marked iron deficiency anaemia. Mr Card sent a letter to Waterford Regional Hospital saying that my bloods were chronic and most likely due to an auto-immune problem.

I was back at Waterford Regional Hospital Outpatients Clinic on 26th May 2005 because I had red eyes; they said it was nodular epic scleritis. I returned to Waterford Regional Hospital on 30th May 2005. I was seen at the outpatient department of Dr Joe Devlin, a rheumatologist consultant. He said that both my barium enema and colonoscopy were inconclusive; the reason for this could not be explained. The rheumatologist felt that as I had a positive rheumatoid factor , it may well be explained by arthritis. Mam asked him about putting me on an iron supplement, and this was prescribed. Here we were now at the end of May, and I had not received the neurologist appointment for Beaumont, so Mam contacted the spina bifida association once again, and they wrote. I then received an appointment in June for 12th December 2006; this was June 2005.

On 11th June 2005, I was admitted for the fourth time following a further seizure; Waterford Regional Hospital recommended the anti-epileptic drugs. On the 12th, Mam spoke with the consultant who was in charge of my care; he told her that I had epilepsy. Mam pleaded with him to transfer me to Beaumont and relayed what Mr Young had said about transferring me should I have another seizure. The consultant said that sending me to Dublin would tell him nothing that he didn't already know, that I was having epileptic fits, and his job was to stop them. Mam was annoyed, and she asked him if it would not be a good idea to have an EEG performed, which would rule in or out epilepsy and decipher what treatment should be given. The doctor declined on the grounds that it would not tell him anything that he did not already know, and his main thing was to put me on tablets to stop me from having seizures.

While I was in the hospital, I had a C.T. scan that showed that there was no significant deterioration in the size of the ventricles. During this admission, the staff was concerned with my low haemoglobin level, which was 8.6, and my iron was 2.9. I also had an upper GI endoscopy which showed that my oesophagus was normal.

By August, I still wasn't very well. Sr Francis, a nursing Mercy nun, often came and sat with me in the afternoon to allow Mam and Dad out for a walk. On this particular day (4th August), when Mam and Dad went out for a walk, Mam fell and damaged her wrist. She could not look after me, so the HSE organised for me to go to a Nursing Home.

I was there for 10 days when a place became available in Claddagh Court, the Wheelchair Association in Kilkenny. I was taken there, and I still wasn't very well, and I was in very bad form. Dad and Mom came to visit me several times, then Mam and Anne McGovern, a great family friend of many years came. Anne comes to Waterford every year especially for my birthday.

No one was able to say what it was or why I was unwell. Mam rang me several times a day, and she could tell something wasn't right. Eventually, on Saturday 3rd September, Dad came for me because I felt I really needed a Doctor; I was in so much pain. Dad had awful trouble getting me into the car because of the pain and stiffness. Mam called the care doctor, and I was given injections for what they thought was acute arthritis.

The following day I was still in terrible pain, and by 6 a.m. on 5th September, I could not reach the phone beside my bed. I could not move my hands or any part of me. The ambulance men were wonderful and gave me gas before they hammocked me out in my own sheet and pillow. I was seeing double, if not treble, by the time they got me into the ambulance.

When I arrived at Waterford Regional Hospital, the casualty SHO wondered if I had Reiter's Syndrome because I presented with red eyes as well as stiffness. She gave Mam sheets of information to read about it. I was given painkillers in casualty, and in the afternoon at about 2.30 p.m. I was admitted into a medical ward, and I was given more painkillers.

On Tuesday morning, 6th September, I was actually crying with pain. When Mam asked at 3.30 p.m. why no doctor was coming to see me, she was told that they were waiting to hand over my care to the rheumatologist and that no one could give me an injection until my chart was handed over. Mam became very annoyed at that, and she demanded that someone come straight away and not to try to play politics with her daughter. So, the doctor came at 3.45 p.m., and I was given an injection for pain. Mam left me at 5 p.m. I texted her as she was driving home to say that I loved her and thanks for getting me the injection.

This was the last time Ingrid used her beloved phone on which she had become an avid texter. Ernie went to visit her at 6.30 p.m., and after him, two nursing nun friends, Sisters Angela and Francis, who left Ingrid at 9 p.m.

10 - DAMAGE, DESPAIR, DECEIT

"Listen to the mother. Mothers know best. It's at your peril if you don't." — PROFESSOR GUINEY

Tragically I must take over the story from here until the end because our precious Ingrid wasn't able to write one more word from this moment onwards. In fact, to all intents and purposes, this was the crucial point that we lost the 'old Ingrid'.

We lost the essence of her, and it was this terrible loss that eventually spurred me on to take legal action on my heroic daughter's behalf. Picking up where Ingrid left off, the course of horrendous events went as follows:

At 9 p.m. on 6th September 2005, Sisters Angela and Francis from the Mercy Order called into our home on their way home from visiting Ingrid. They had a nightdress that needed washing, and they brought it to me. All four of us sat in the conservatory having tea and discussing Ingrid and the nuns left just after ten. I decided to check on Ingrid before going to bed, but there was no answer from the phone at the ward. I thought that perhaps the nurses couldn't answer the phone because some unfortunate soul was in trouble and needed attention so decided to go to bed hoping Ingrid was sleeping peacefully.

Early next morning, I phoned to check how Ingrid was, and the male nurse in charge said, "not well." He explained that Ingrid had had a very bad seizure just before 10 p.m. and had nearly died. I was speechless! I went to Waterford Regional Hospital, which was 10 minutes from our home, to find Ingrid in a coma and in a very bad state. I was told that at 9.45 p.m. the previous night, the patient in the next bed to Ingrid who happened to be a nurse had gone to the nurse's station saying that Ingrid was grunting. When they arrived at her bedside, Ingrid was fitting, had vomited, and her eyes were fixed and dilated. The nursing staff rang a doctor and an intern arrived - he rang for the next in line, a senior house officer who came to see Ingrid at 10.15 p.m. At this stage Ingrid had been fitting for 25–30 minutes. By the time the medical registrar saw her, he recorded that Ingrid had been fitting for 25–40 minutes. Ingrid remained unconscious. The timeline here in stopping her seizure and lack of oxygen is where I believe it all started to go wrong.

I was Ingrid's mother and throughout the ordeal tried to share my opinion on what I thought was happening to her and why. I had watched as she endured numerous infections, setbacks, operations and recoveries for 34 long years which I felt warranted that I be listened to. However, time and again my words fell on deaf ears.

I wanted her to be put onto Claforan at this point because that's what I remembered she had previously responded well to in Beaumont.

I also specifically told them in Waterford Hospital not to give her Difene because I remembered all too well that she had a bad reaction to it before. I suspected that something within anti-inflammatories could be worsening or even causing the seizures.

Despite my pleas, Ingrid was given Difene! She was given three doses and Ingrid was in a seizure for almost an hour. By this stage, they had given her so much sedation that she was in an induced coma, and the anaesthetist was going to put her on life support.

Not one of them on that day would have inspired any confidence in the health service in that hospital. I was beside myself with worry, frustration and anger. I was devastated that the hospital had not called me to let me know how serious Ingrid's condition was and so that I could be by her side but was also frustrated and angry at the decisions taken related to her care in that crucial period when she was really struggling.

From here on, Ingrid had a 24-hour watch carried out by extended family and friends. On Thursday morning, an anaesthetist review was requested, and he decided to give Ingrid a drug to reverse the effect of sedation, after which she slowly opened her eyes. Ingrid remained very drowsy, but she could be given sips of oral fluid through a straw. I was very concerned from the time Ingrid opened her eyes and tried to speak because it was very clear she was not right. She could not focus, she was not aware of her surroundings, she could not identify who was with her, and she was very confused. Just by looking at her, I knew that she didn't have a clue what was going on. Graham was at home at the time and confirmed my worst fear when he took one look at her and said, "Mam, Ingrid's brain-damaged!"

I kept thinking to myself, "We live minutes from this hospital! We were lying in our beds, and our daughter was close to dying a stone's throw away from us!" I just could not accept or understand why they hadn't phoned us.

I screamed at them, "Were you going to call us if she had died?"

The doctor calmly insisted she was just confused because of the amount of sedation she was given, and she was still running a temperature and might have an infection. Her condition continued to deteriorate over the following days; IV fluids were re-commenced, and she was started on an antibiotic. A chest x-ray was ordered as they thought she might have aspirated. She was then seen by the on-call team as she had a seizure that lasted 10 minutes, and she lost consciousness for another 20 minutes. The consultant continued to say that Ingrid would be fine in three weeks, yet Ingrid continued to deteriorate. I was advised by a staff member to take Ingrid to Dublin. That staff member knew how arrogant the consultant was and how wrongly the entire episode had been handled and understood that taking Ingrid to Beaumont where the doctors could treat her with a clean slate, would provide her only chance of any recovery. However, I also distinctly remember my heart sinking when the same person whispered sympathetically, "It's probably too late now."

This person knew how things sat. This person knew Ingrid had brain damage, and this person knew they had been negligent. She had seen it all with her own eyes. I had stood there nearly pulling my hair out while an anaesthetist and a registrar debated whether to give Ingrid a drug to reverse the sedation and risk a further seizure or not. Time was ticking and from where I was standing no one seemed capable of making a decision quick enough.

By Sunday 18th September, 12 days after Ingrid's initial brain injury, I was at the end of my tether, so I wrote a letter to the neurosurgeon at Beaumont, pleading with him to come on board and save Ingrid. I asked Waterford Regional Hospital to fax it from the hospital, and they did so. The neurosurgeon's registrar, rang the hospital and suggested to them that Ingrid have a central line inserted to facilitate the change of antibiotic to Claforan, the drug I had suggested. On 20th September, Tuesday night, Ingrid was taken to surgery for this procedure. This antibiotic, given through the central line, clearly began to work. Over the next couple of days, Ingrid did show some physical and outward signs of improvement. By Thursday afternoon, a bed became available in Beaumont and Ingrid was transferred there by ambulance. Her brother Gordon went in the ambulance with Ingrid, and her Dad and I followed in the car.

Ingrid remained in Beaumont for four weeks, where they continued to give her the Claforan. Ingrid's physical condition improved slightly, but her mental state did not. After four weeks of every medical test imaginable, carried out by the neuro team, they reached the conclusion that there was nothing more they could do for Ingrid as her brain had been damaged prior to her admission to Beaumont. We were informed that Waterford had been "out of their depth and should have off-loaded Ingrid sooner."

Ingrid spent her 35th birthday on the high dependency ward. Graham and Gordon were both there. I remember it was football season and the boys kept running in and out to catch up on a match on the TV. Ingrid had received a lovely candle from Medjugorje. At one stage I heard a barely audible voice coming from Ingrid and when I looked, she had bitten a chunk out of the candle. This just shows how far gone she was at this point.

It was suggested a nursing home for Ingrid as it was felt that we couldn't possibly manage her at home. Beaumont found it very hard saying this to us. We asked to have her transferred back to Waterford.

With heavy hearts, we left Beaumont on Thursday 20th October 2005 to travel back to Waterford Regional Hospital, Ingrid doing so by ambulance where she was readmitted. Her stay this time in Waterford was anything but pleasant. Due to understaffing, the care was appalling. The HSE were working on putting a care package in place, but it was taking too long, and Ingrid's care was too important to us. Ingrid's short-term memory was nil, so she couldn't tell if anyone had been to attend to her or not or if she had eaten a meal or drank anything. Ingrid spent 16 nights in Waterford from 20th October to 5th November. The consultant who told us that Ingrid would be fine in three weeks never came to visit Ingrid or us again.

We would be there every single day in the hospital doing everything we could to make Ingrid's experience comfortable. I recall a certain medication had affected Ingrid's teeth very badly. Ingrid had always had lovely teeth, but the medication had made them black. Ernie used to stand in that hospital with the electric toothbrush and brush Ingrid's teeth meticulously several times a day. One day a woman said to him, "I'm watching you do that every day and I don't know many others that would have the same dedication." Ernie turned to her and simply said, "She's my daughter, what do you want me to do?!"

It was as simple as that; Ernie would have done anything in this world for Ingrid. She was his precious beloved little girl.

When we got her home, we gradually got Ingrid back to eating food herself, brushing her teeth, getting on and off the bed (with great difficulty) and getting in and out of the shower. These were all things that she could do very well prior to September, the basic everyday tasks of life but now we had to re-teach them to her. It was an arduous task that took time and patience, but we could see small improvements over time. Christmas of that year wasn't a great one. As a family, we were all here, her two brothers, her dad and me. To see Ingrid opening the same present, again and again, was heart-breaking. We all rallied around and supported each other and Ingrid as best as we could, and we survived. We realised how very lucky we were to have Ingrid alive and with us at home at Christmas. We tried to get Ingrid doing as much for herself as possible. We started helping her put her tablets in the appropriate container every week. Ingrid became very proficient at this and would know if one was missing or looked different to how it should. Ingrid knew this was 'her' job and performed it with precision and enthusiasm, spurred on by our constant encouragement and motivation.

Ingrid was clearly traumatised by her ordeal in hospital and once home would wake numerous times each night calling out in the dark for someone to come and comfort her. Looking back, I wonder how we got through it, getting up seven or eight times in the night every night. Eventually we employed a nurse called Sarah to help and at long last we got a full night's sleep.

In January 2006, we returned to Beaumont with Ingrid to visit the neurosurgeon, and his first words to Ingrid were, "Well, I only have to look at you to know that you were at home." He was very pleased with how well she looked and how much better she was physically, but he could see how much ground was lost mentally.

We continued to help Ingrid in any way we could. She had to rest daily as she tired very easily, napping sometimes for up to two and a half hours after lunch, and she couldn't be left on her own at any stage. The team from Acquired Brain Injury Ireland came on board with advice, and their support was a great help. A lady in the hospital contacted this team and they visited Ingrid in hospital at first and then checked in on her at home.

It certainly was a full-time job looking after the new Ingrid. The old Ingrid that could stay at home alone, answer the door, phone and entertain whoever called was no more. I learned this the hard way. One morning I dropped her dad off at the bus stop. I was gone for 10–15 minutes. I returned to find Ingrid in tears and shaking with fear as she thought she was abandoned and did not know how she would manage. Never again was she left alone in the house, even for a second.

Ingrid celebrating our 40th wedding anniversary with her characteristic smile, 2006

11 - PROFESSORS, POETRY, PROCEEDINGS

The years after Ingrid's brain injury were very tough years but also very rewarding ones. Ingrid seemed happy, and as long as there was a smile on her face most of the time, which was all we needed to keep the rest of us happy.

Ingrid went on short respite breaks to the Cheshire home in Co Wicklow. At one stage Jarlath, the manager of Cheshire Home in Ardeen, Shillelagh Co. Wicklow asked me to go to a HSE board meeting where they were trying to put the pressure on to get a similar home built in Waterford. I did so and brought Ingrid along to voice her opinion and share how valuable she thought it would be. This was built on the grounds of St. Patrick's Hospital. Ingrid went there on respite and she eventually was offered a full time place there. She declined this saying she was very happy at home and not ready to leave.

In 2006 we arranged a special evening to celebrate Ingrid's physical recovery from her brain injury. We wrote to Prof. Guiney, and he made the trip to Waterford to attend. We offered to chauffeur him personally, but he wouldn't hear of it. We didn't tell Ingrid a thing about him coming and when she set eyes on him in the chapel the surprise on her face was priceless. Ingrid's firm friends Bishop Russell and Father Liddane celebrated mass in Ballygunner Church and we then went to the Tower Hotel for refreshments. A family friend Seosamh MacGearailt, who visited Ingrid every Sunday, performed a poem that he wrote himself:

'Against The Odds'

They said she wouldn't make it,
I'm so glad they got it
wrong. But God created such a
spirit That's inspired us for so
long.
She defied the odds from day
one Overcoming all thrown at
her. She puts her demons on the
run With no little bother.
In Cheshire's Home, she said it all,
I was privileged to hear her say,
"Am I not the lucky one
To be as good as I am today"?
Her lovely smile disarms us all,
Encouraging those around her.
In wheelchair small, she still walks tall
No barrier can contain her.
Her glass is full, though some think not,
She stands up to the measure.
So, thank you, Lord, for what she's got
And for Ingrid, 'Our Special Treasure'.

By Seosamh MacGearailt, 6th October 2006

I drove Professor Guiney back to the train station the next day after his visit, and he told me it was very fortunate that Ingrid had been born in 1970 because in 1972, the 'selective method' would have been implied and Ingrid would not have had the opportunity to survive and thrive as she did. This meant that a child with Spina Bifida would have been left for a few months without any intervention, and if they lived, only then would an operation have been considered. This struck such a chord with me when I thought how easily we might not have had Ingrid in this world or our lives. That, for me, was an unbearable thought. He said the medical team felt it was a very onerous task to ask of parents as everyone couldn't do what we did. As I said to him then, we would not have been without even one second of her life.

In 2006, I made a huge decision, which I did not tell a soul about at the time. I decided to approach a solicitor about Ingrid's mistreatment in Waterford Hospital. I believed she had been rendered unnecessarily brain damaged by an inept system and poor decision making. I was prepared to fight, and I was prepared to go to court to see justice done.

I contacted Cantillon's' Law Practice in Cork '.

This kick-started an extremely lengthy process, which saw senior partners Pat Daly and Ernest Cantillon send Ingrid and I for a litany of consultations with neurologists as far afield as London. As a family we went to hell and back.

For every consultation we attended on the request of our insurers we had to attend others on the request of the opposition (HSE). I remember walking out of one such appointment that had been organised by the HSE and thinking to myself, we're on the right track! Ironically, I had been forewarned that the particular neurologist I was going to see was unfavourable to say the least. Our appointment was for 9am. I had booked Ingrid her dad and myself into the Hilton Hotel and booked a wheelchair taxi to ensure we would be on time. We were still sitting waiting at 11am and I thought I was going to explode. I was terrified Ingrid would have a seizure. The first thing this supposedly infamous man did when he met us was apologise. Further to his credit he then came from behind his desk and came over to Ingrid and spoke to her at her level. He asked Ingrid to do several tasks, some of which she could do and others she could not. We were with him for a good hour and he was a complete gentleman. At the end of the appointment, he said that Ingrid was 'one of the worst amnesiacs he'd ever come across'. He was very taken with Ingrid and as we left the room, he said to me, 'All I can do is wish you the very best, you are wonderful parents.' On this day when I phoned Cantillon's I said to them, 'I honestly think we are halfway there.'

Ingrid with Joseph Fitzgerald - aka Seosamh MacGearailt, the author of 'Against The Odds' - and his wife Vera

Ingrid at her special night with Professor Guiney

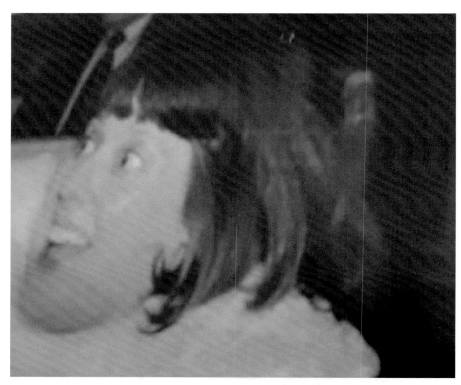

*Ingrid's reaction to seeing Prof Guiney
at her special night*

12 - THE NEW INGRID

Statements of fact about Ingrid's character were also gathered from various people who knew, taught and were inspired by her at various stages of her life. Each of these statements reinforced just how much of the old Ingrid we had lost due to her brain injury. What all these people had in common was not only the love they had for Ingrid but also their appreciation of her unique and clever mind, which had deteriorated dramatically since her seizures began.

I have included excerpts from these statements to reinforce the magnitude of the loss we felt when our social butterfly Ingrid emerged from her coma, a shadow of her former flighty self. These statements highlight the extent of Ingrid's skills base, her impeccable interpersonal skills and her tireless ability to inform and entertain at every turn.

Joseph Fitzgerald (68), retired Production Planner

I am a family friend of the Walsh family. My wife and Mary Walsh, Ingrid's mother, were childhood neighbours. Whilst we have known the Walsh family throughout our lives, it was not until later years that I became a regular caller to the Walsh family home.

I have, from time to time, interviewed local people who I felt had a story to tell and that should be recorded for posterity. I felt that Ingrid had a story that should be preserved, and therefore, over two evenings, I recorded Ingrid's story on two

CDs entitled Ingrid 1 and Ingrid 2. My tapes are dated March/April 2005. In addition, on listening to the tape in Ingrid 1, she states that she is approaching her 35th birthday, 25th September, which corroborates that this recording was made in March/April 2005.

It will be apparent from those recordings that Ingrid was able to give a clear and precise account of her life story and experiences, as will be evident from the tapes. I was also on the Board of Management of St Paul's Secondary School, where Ingrid attended. I heard that Ingrid had addressed the students at the Presentation Convent. I mentioned this to Anthony Russell, the Headmaster of St Paul's, and he invited Ingrid to attend the school and talk to the students about her disability. I sat in on the lecture, and it will be clear from the tapes that Ingrid was a natural communicator.

She coped with life's adversities in terms of her disability with a smile on her face. The students were enthralled and thanked the teachers profusely for organising the event.

At Anthony Russell's retirement, he invited Ingrid to attend. When a Headmaster retires, he can make a 'Principal's Award'. He said that the reason he had chosen Ingrid was that he admired Ingrid's personality, in that she showed tenacity in dealing with the challenges of her disability.

It is with much sadness that I now visit the Walsh home. I try to do so on a weekly basis in order to give Mary and Ernie a break. I sit with Ingrid; however, her short-term memory is now so poor that the conversation becomes circular; it is as if she is on a loop. I find it a tragedy that the one thing that Ingrid had in her life was her unique ability to communicate and socialise with others. Unfortunately, this skill has now been eroded following the severe fit in September 2005.

Maura Donoghue (56), Tipperary, a teacher at the Presentation Secondary School , Waterford

I had a child with spina bifida (who is now deceased), and I met Ingrid through the Spina Bifida Society.

If you knew Ingrid prior to her brain injury, it would have been apparent that she was a good communicator.

In my capacity as a teacher, I was in charge of the senior certificate students up until 2003 and part of the senior students' course was a social education programme. As part of that programme, I introduced the students to disability, and I felt, given Ingrid's social/communication skills, that she would be a very effective speaker as part of that module of the course. I invited Ingrid to attend in order to address the students about her disability, and I believe that she did it for five or six years. The last year she addressed the students was in 2003, which was the final year that I was in charge of the Senior Certificate course.

Ingrid's talk to the students was about her birth, her life living with a disability and the impact that it had on her in terms of integration. She was such a good communicator that she had the ability to hold the class enthralled. They were all fascinated by her, and it was a testament to her that when the bell went, the students did not move but would stay glued to hear what she had to say.

As a teacher who needs to communicate effectively, I was fascinated by Ingrid's skill of being able to get her message across. Whilst she was talking about disability, she was able to interweave the story with so much emotion and humour that I envied her skill.

Following my talk, my students were always thankful for Ingrid's input in that as part of the course, they had to do a project on disability. Ingrid's talk was always so much more beneficial than any classroom-based work that I could do.

In that, Ingrid was telling the story from the perspective of the person dealing with a disability, and that way, she made it real. A thank you card was given to Ingrid by a student of mine by the name of Ann-Marie Byrne following Ingrid's last talk at the school. I am able to say that Ann-Marie heard Ingrid speak in 2003, as it was in the last class that I taught.

I was extremely saddened at a recent meeting with Ingrid to experience, first-hand, the profound deterioration of Ingrid's memory/recall. She no longer knew who I was, nor was she able to effectively hold a conversation with me.

Paddy Power, retired principal of St Saviour's National School (Primary School), Waterford

In my capacity as headmaster, I was contacted by Ingrid Walsh's parents in 1983 and asked whether or not I would be prepared to enrol Ingrid in my school. It was explained to me that she had profound physical disabilities as a result of spina bifida and that she was in a wheelchair. She had attended primary school at St John of God's School, but the building of the school was on two floors and could not accommodate Ingrid's disability as Ingrid was required to transfer upstairs.

My school was not completely disability- friendly in that it was not specifically built with disabled children in mind. Nonetheless, it was all on the flat, and there was access out of each classroom via French doors onto a patio that accommodated Ingrid's entry and exit from the school.

Because of Ingrid's disability and hospitalisations, she missed a lot of schooling at St John of Gods, and she was apparently 'below' her peers. However, as far as I was concerned, my philosophy with education is that you take the child from where they are, you do not measure the child according to their peers, and you can see if you can bring that child on.

On admitting Ingrid into the school, it was clear that she had intelligence. If Ingrid did not have intelligence, I would have asked for a psychological report to be carried out and then would have referred Ingrid to a special school.

It was clear to her teachers and me that Ingrid had intelligence and that the biggest handicap in her life was the physical disabilities imposed on her by spina bifida. Ingrid had immense social skills, and initially, I had some reservations. Given Ingrid's background and that she had attended St John of God's school, which was probably the most socially acceptable school, and St Saviour's was the most socially disadvantaged school in Waterford, it could have repercussions. However, Ingrid's social skills were so warm and friendly that the children not only loved her, but they looked after her. (I have given this as an example of Ingrid's sociability, but I would not like to say anything about the social standing of my former school in evidence.) From 1983 to 1985, during the time that Ingrid attended St Saviour's, there was no such thing as an SNA (Special Needs Assistant). We did have a special room for Ingrid, and either Mrs Walsh or a nurse would come and deal with Ingrid's toilet needs.

In the time that Ingrid was with us, she made credible progress. She was never going to be an intellectual, but my aspiration for Ingrid was that we would be able to equip her with sufficient skills to be able to be a useful member of society. Ingrid progressed from St Saviour's School to St Paul's Secondary School. I used to keep an eye on Ingrid's progress and get reports from my sister, Eileen, the home economics teacher at St Paul's, who taught Ingrid domestic science at secondary level. Ingrid did her Group Certificate in domestic science. Eileen informed me that Ingrid's biggest disadvantage, in terms of her education, was her physical disability, which impeded her, especially in the domestic science setting.

Anthony Russell (67), retired Headmaster of St Paul's Community College

I had been principal of that school for 24 years until I retired in 2002. In that time, I put a number of students through my hands as the school had a maximum capacity of 900 pupils. I recall Ingrid Walsh extremely well because of her sunny disposition and her vivacious personality.

Whilst Ingrid was never going to achieve brilliance in terms of academia, in that she would not have an honours Leaving certificate. Nonetheless, she had intelligence. At the college, we had a banding option, whereby we would offer students a

Group Certificate over three years if they wanted to. They could then progress up to Intermediate Certificate and Leaving Certificate thereafter. This suited a number of students at the school, and we geared Ingrid towards that option.

Evelyn Waters, Counsellor Therapist with the National Counselling Service o f HSE

From 1992 to 1995, I was employed as a Skills Foundation Instructor at Rehab in Waterford. Rehab is now called the National Training and Development Institution. In that capacity, I used to run the Level 1 Skills Foundation Course for adults who suffered from physical and intellectual disabilities. Ingrid Walsh joined the course and became a student of mine.

There were about 10–15 students in her group who would have had various intellectual and physical disabilities.

Some members of the group would also have behavioural problems associated with their learning disability. Ingrid did not have any intellectual or behavioural problems; her challenges were associated with her physical ability. The course consisted of 50% practical skills, sampling of the work environment, which included catering, sewing, upholstery, and office administration, and 50% classroom- based activities, whereby I would teach the students about social work-based skills, including how to prepare a CV, how to respond to a job advertisement and how to fill in various forms.

We had computers in the classroom, and Ingrid gained proficiency in using the particular software. There were various times during the classroom-based activities where my attention would be taken up in dealing with the more challenging behaviour of some of the students. Ingrid was self-sufficient, and I could leave her to work away on her own. Ingrid would tell me various stories about her life, and I suggested to her that if she wrote a book, it would become a bestseller. Ingrid then began to write her life story on theclassroom computer and we would review it together.

In 1993, Ingrid had shunt surgery in Beaumont, and I recall that we were all concerned about her. However, when she returned, it was evident to all concerned that she had made a recovery, and I can confirm that there did not appear to be any intellectual deficit; the same bright and bubbly Ingrid returned following the surgery if a little tired.

As part of the course, there would be a multi-disciplinary meeting that included input from a psychologist. At those meetings, we would draw up a plan for the student going forward. In terms of the practical skills sampling course, catering and upholstery training were not considered a suitable option for Ingrid because of her physical disability. However, she showed potential in the office administration area. As part of the administration work, another trainee used to man our reception area, whereby she would answer the phone and meet and greet visitors.

Ingrid had highly advanced social skills, and her personality was ideal for receptionist work, and she excelled in that environment. As a result, I had hopes that Ingrid would have been able to pursue a career in an administrative environment.

While Ingrid could have progressed to Level Two of the Skills Foundation Course at Rehab, we recognised that the courses we offered were not a match for her abilities. So, I encouraged her to apply to Waterford Regional College for the Mature Students Foundation Course. Unfortunately, the Rehab records are no longer available, but I have been shown a copy of the letter that I wrote to a Nurse O'Sullivan, dated October 1994, from which it will be apparent that I recorded that Ingrid had progressed from our service to Waterford Regional College and we were very pleased with her success. I can confirm that I would deem Ingrid as one of Rehab's success stories.

Seamus McGrath (56), Chief Clerk at Waterford Circuit Court for the past 24 years

My daughter Deirdre was a friend of Ingrid Walsh at school, and I met Ingrid through Deirdre. In my capacity as Court Clerk, I have responsibility for running the local, national and European elections. I am also responsible for appointing polling clerks for the polling stations. It was apparent to me that Ingrid had the necessary intellect to carry out the duties of a poll clerk, and I thought that she might be interested. Therefore, I approached her about becoming a Polling Clerk. Ingrid readily agreed. She officiated at St Martin's School in Waterford, which was fully equipped to deal with disability, and therefore, it was an ideal location for Ingrid to officiate.

To my recollection, Ingrid was a Polling Clerk for 15 years.

The position of Polling Clerk is an arduous task in that it is, first of all, a demanding long day as they are usually at stations between 12 and 14 hours. In addition, the Polling Clerk has to be responsible for checking off the public's voting cards with the register and challenging various people as necessary with regard to identification, etc. Ingrid coped marvellously with the job in hand and had a very nice manner with the public. Ingrid became very well known by the voters at St Martin's, who used to greet her warmly.

When the electronic voting machines were brought in, Ingrid attended the study day and was trained in their use. When Ingrid got paid, she used that money she got from officiating at the polling station to bring her mother and father to dinner. They used to go to a restaurant called O'Dwyer's on Mary Street, which was run by a well-known restaurateur by the name of Martin O'Dwyer.

13 - COURTS, CARE, CONFIDANTS

In 2009, on the night before the scheduled court case arrived, Liam Reidy SC and David Holland SC battled it out with the opposition in the High Court, they in one room and we in another, next door. Several settlement amounts were bandied about during negotiations that evening. Despite the figures rising exponentially, we were continually told that the amount awarded could be significantly higher if it went to Court.

A common tactic employed by hospitals and doctors sued for clinical negligence (but also common practice in many other areas of tort law) is to only engage in negotiations with the injured party 1 or 2 days before the trial is due to begin, effectively on the steps of the courthouse. It is a commonly employed tactic which is grossly unfair to the injured parties as they have to prepare to testify in court and must emotionally and physically invest in and prepare themselves for a very difficult trial that will delve into the character and history of the victim and force the family to relive the most difficult times of their lives. This practice may serve a purpose for the HSE and their insurers but is grossly unfair to victims.

However, we were also acutely aware that we were in danger of getting less or nothing if we went to court and ultimately the process and award was about ensuring and securing Ingrid's future. Graham wanted to go to court as he felt they should accept negligence and apologise, but for Ernie and me, it really was about just getting enough to secure Ingrid's private care.

In the end, we settled for €2.5 million. I had a piece ready for any journalists that might be outside the court that day, but there weren't any. I would simply have thanked Cantillon's for their guidance before saying publicly, "This settlement will enable us to afford the kind of professional care Ingrid so deserves as someone who fought to live all her life only to be brain damaged through no fault of her own. The essence of Ingrid is what we miss the most, and no amount of money can bring that back."

I am delighted to say that our daughter Ingrid lived for another 14 years after her brain injury, so the money she received for her care had to last.

I fought tooth and nail for her in a long lengthy battle against a sickening two-tiered system. A lying cloak-and-dagger, dog-eat-dog secretive system where everyone looks after each other and everyone scratches each other's back to the detriment of the poor ill-informed and mistreated citizens who put their trust in these systems daily. I am well aware that we only got where we did because we had money to start. I want to encourage anyone reading this book who may not have the luxury of money. I feel genuinely so, so sorry for you. I can only hope that somehow you will keep using what you do have: your voice and your individual right to speak up and speak out for what is right to fight for justice. Shout loud enough, and I, for one, will be hoping and praying that somehow, your plea will fall on the right ears, and you will get some sort of peace for your family.

It took four years for the court case to come, and in that time, I felt like I went to hell and back. I discovered just how easily mistakes get made and how quickly innocent family members can become scapegoats.

In many ways, I feel the system has improved, but in many areas, I fear it has not. For example, Ingrid never had to go on a waiting list in her early years. When I think of young people with scoliosis today, some are waiting upwards of four years for an operation. Now that is disgraceful!

In 2008 we applied and received planning for a bungalow at the top of our back garden. The bungalow was purpose built to meet Ingrid's needs. It consisted of two bedrooms, two bathrooms, a kitchen-cum- living room, utility room, and a sitting room. The idea was when we had nurses/carers employed they had their own space and Ingrid had her ensuite room with all facilities.

Thank God we had this space as a few years earlier we had to fight to retain what was rightfully ours. When we purchased our site in 1974 it went way back. We were only able to cultivate half of it at first and the back part was a wilderness. In the 90s it came to my attention that planning permission was sought to build there as well as an adjoining green area that the City Council had sold to a City Builder. A long disagreement ensued which had a very favourable outcome. City Council eventually graciously apologised, saying they had pulled a bloomer and Land Registry had compounded it by changing our deeds. This is where Ingrid's beautiful bungalow was built with the loveliest garden that was her tranquil space.

One of the best things we did was build that house and Ingrid spent many happy years there.

We employed private nurses to help with Ingrid's care. The first came in 2008 before the Court Case, a Nigerian lady called Sarah who ended up referring to me as her 'Irish mammy'.

We laughed heartily one day not long after she started with us. Obviously, English wasn't her first language, so when she spoke to Ingrid for the first time, it was in heavily accented English. She said, "Ingrid, my name is Sarah. I'm here to help Mam to look after you." On hearing this, Ingrid piped up, "If you are going to look after me, you will have to learn how to speak proper English!"

So, a baptism of fire was for Sarah into life with Ingrid. Thankfully, she saw the funny side, and from that moment on, they got on like a house on fire.

On another occasion, a lovely doctor from Care Doc had come to see Ingrid in our home. He noticed our lovely conservatory and started chatting to me about how much his wife wanted one. As we chatted and I happily answered his questions, Ingrid piped up from the other room, "Tell me this, did you come to see the conservatory or me?!" Thankfully, he just laughed it off. Her sense of humour was something else! I remember times when she was really very unwell, and I would be chatting to her nurses, and she would interrupt with, "I could be dead over here for all you two would know!" She was someone who always made sure no one stayed too downcast around her.

I don't like to make exceptions when it comes to extolling the virtues of Ingrid's nurses and carers but there was one that was exactly that, exceptional. This was Geraldine, or as we called her Ger. Ger was Ingrid's only carer, the rest were nurses. She came on board in 2010 and cared for Ingrid for 9 years. A mother to four sons she used to say that Ingrid was the daughter she never had. Ger and I got very close and she got to know just how meticulous I was about writing everything down. I had notebooks piled high charting all Ingrid's hospital stays and what happened during them. Everywhere I went I would have a notebook and pen handy to make notes. Ger has thanked me recently for inspiring her to do the same as she battles her own illness. Ger went out sick herself the year Ingrid died. She was something else! Rain, hail or snow she was there and filled in so many times when others couldn't make it. We will be eternally grateful to her. Ger lost her battle on 12th August, 2022. Rest in Peace, Ger, your memory lives on.

Even with her awful seizures, Ingrid was never ever fearful. Nor did she lose her ability for empathy and compassion. Sometimes we were reminded of this the hard way. Ingrid had been a huge Michael Jackson fan. After her brain injury, we had to be so careful that she didn't hear that he had died on the TV. Her memory was practically non- existent, so every time she discovered Michael Jackson was dead, it was like she was hearing it for the first time. It was like Michael Jackson died again, and again and again! And each time she made the fateful discovery, the tears would pour down her face, and she would be inconsolable.

Other ways that we knew Ingrid still had the profound gift of listening down to an art was when the stories would come flooding in about how she had listened, advised and hugged nurses through the night who had shared their worries with her. In 2018, one such nurse came to me after spending the night with Ingrid and said, "Ingrid was my rock last night." The nurse had spent the weekend crying because her lovely son had told her something that she really didn't feel she could cope with. Ingrid sensed there was something wrong and said to her, "You need a hug. Come on, tell me all about it. I have two shoulders. Give it to me. I can handle it!" While hugging her, the nurse told Ingrid everything. While hugging and tapping her shoulder affectionately, Ingrid said, "Your son doesn't need your tears. He needs your support. Your son is going to be OK. Take a look at me sitting here. I wouldn't be here today if it weren't for my mam and dad taking such good care of me and loving and supporting me."

I spoke to that nurse recently, and she remembered that night when Ingrid was her 'rock' and Ingrid was, of course, right – everything worked out fine.

She was praising me to high heaven on the phone, which I struggled to listen to. She insisted, "You carried the can, Mary. You and Ernie created Ingrid, and she was exceptional!"

I was embarrassed and said, "Oh, come on now, stop it!" Then the following day, I went to Mass, and the priest was quoting verses from the gospels that were encouraging humility and modesty. I laughed. It was like God was making sure I didn't get above my station!

14 - NEGLECT, NOTICE, NOTES

The court battle wasn't the only battle I fought for my daughter. In 2007 I had to undergo surgery, and Ingrid was put into a Care Home in Waterford during this time. Ingrid's stay was subsidised by the disability section of the HSE, as would be typical in such a situation. Unfortunately, things didn't go to plan with my procedure, and I ended up staying longer in hospital and having a more difficult and lengthy recovery than originally anticipated. This meant that Ingrid had to stay in the home longer than planned. Because of my surgery the physical lifting and manoeuvring of Ingrid was too difficult. I had access to visit Ingrid, however, at any time and observed first hand the level of care provided to residents within the Home.

Unfortunately, that level of care in that place at times was horrendous. The home was understaffed and the staff overworked or ill-prepared to deal with any patients who needed a relatively high level of care. On one occasion, I witnessed my daughter being carried out of the shower naked with absolutely no consideration given to her dignity. I also discovered faeces on the floor on a number of occasions and even worse, I found prescription tablets that Ingrid should have taken in a bedside drawer (tablets that were extremely important to her health). The list of unacceptable practices that I observed became longer and longer as the days went on.

I was already going into the home to catheterise Ingrid any time there was a male member of staff on duty at night as by law a male is not allowed to catheterise a female (this at least was a legal requirement at the time in Ireland and may still be although I do not believe the reverse is enshrined in law i.e. that a female cannot catheterise a male). When I looked to address this with the nursing manager when admitting Ingrid, I was told that the home could not ensure a female nurse would always be available in the evening to catheterise Ingrid before she went to sleep. The best the home could do was to put extra sheets underneath Ingrid to soak up her pee and maybe prevent it getting through to the bed clothes. Needless to say, having Ingrid sleep in soaking wet sheets with a wet blanket underneath her was not an option for us and not a suggestion I took favourably to.

I ended up being the person the staff looked to learn how best to handle Ingrid's needs and care and to deal with her catheterisation. When I was not there to catheterise Ingrid, it could typically be a very long time before she was changed and on a number of occasions I arrived at the Home to find her soaking wet, having not been changed for many hours. A bell that Ingrid was meant to use to call for assistance was stuck down the back of her bedside cabinet and she could not reach it. The awful thing about this is that on one occasion a number of days previously, a staff member told me that Ingrid was pushing the bell so often (asking for them to 'change' - catheterise her) that they were tempted to put it out of her reach.

I complained directly to the care home about all of these observations, expecting and hoping that it may lead to some improvement in the level of care provided to Ingrid. I received no direct response from the Home whatsoever. Rather than apologising and fixing the situation, they contacted Community Care (who were part funding Ingrid's stay) to complain about me and my behaviour! In addition, after consulting Community Care they gave Ingrid notice to leave the home and ask that she be removed within a month. The nursing home was of the opinion that Ingrid should go to a different home. Needless to say, we took her home to make sure she was looked after properly.

I discovered the Home had contacted Community Care to tell them that I didn't always act in Ingrid's best interests and she should go to a different Nursing Home. There was no evidence or detail offered to back up this claim but it was submitted and taken seriously by the Community Care team. It was quite unbelievable but what happened next was almost worse! The Community Care admin office who had never met Ingrid or any one of her family, friends or doctors, sat at a desk together and decided to refer Ingrid to the Vulnerable Adults Office. This was done without even a call to Ingrid's G.P. which should have been the first port of call. The letter of the 8th April 2009 to the Team leader of Vulnerable Adults outlined the concern of Disability Services Community Care to Ingrid's parents both pensioners caring for her with very little support hours available from the HSE. Thankfully, the VAC did not take this referral seriously, as it did not meet any threshold they had for referral (which is based on abuse or neglect) - in fact the VAC never even responded to Community Care; they were likely extremely confused as to why Ingrid was referred to them at all.

That said, I was devastated to find this out. I only discovered this event and many more when I requested notes under the Freedom of Information and I also contacted the Office of the Ombudsman (who was wonderful and very supportive). I received internal emails, correspondence etc. to various departments within Community Care. As I went through all this material, I began to uncover a litany of blatant untruths and an attitude of self-preservation that trumped everything else. One such saying I refused to allow Ingrid to go to hospital when a doctor felt she should go. This was very upsetting for me to read and plainly inaccurate I was subsequently able (and felt forced) to prove where the doctor said there was no need for her to go. It was appalling to read that a consultant had written requesting a visit to Ingrid from a Public Health Nurse (PHN) that Community Care instructed their nurses not to visit our home. (for reasons that are to this day unclear to me)

The Ombudsman also confirmed to me in writing that a senior investigator raised the issue of retrospective entries being added to Ingrid's notes for 2009 in 2011 with the HSE Community Care (as you can imagine this is very much a forbidden practice in medicine and care, given the ability of someone to rewrite history with the benefit of hindsight)

I complained to the Director of Nursing on the 19th May, and received a letter informing me I would not hear back until the 2nd of July (which seemed a very specific date in the future) – their response was sent on the 2nd, but not received by me until the 3rd of July. The team's answer to my letter about the nursing home (almost seven weeks later) told me that, as of July 1st, they no longer had the authority to investigate complaints against nursing homes and I was instead advised to contact HIQA with my complaint. This I did, and found HIQA were only authorised to investigate complaints on behalf of current nursing home residents. That same letter went missing and when I requested the Ombudsman to have it added to Ingrid's notes, I was asked if a copy could be given to Community Care, as they had mysteriously misplaced the original. To me it felt like there was a lot of subterfuge at play to effectively make me go forget about or ultimately drop any complaint or grievance I felt. The most disappointing aspect is that the staff was actually told (in writing) that if I was not happy with a particular outcome and continued to ask questions, the Vexatious Client Policy may be pursued.

The biggest irony and most damaging part of this whole sorry episode was that despite classing Ingrid as 'a vulnerable adult' and referring her to the VAC, not one person from the HSE/Community Care had come anywhere near us or our home to assess Ingrid's care or speak to her or us. The scary truth was that had she actually been vulnerable or in need of help, she never would have received it.

Two years after that letter of referral to the Vulnerable Adults outlining their concern, I asked the Ombudsman what transpired. An email sent by the Ombudsman to Community Care asked them what had happened and how this matter was followed up and an email was sent to the Team Leader who received the referral. His reply of 18th April 2011 over two years later stated simply this referral did not meet the threshold for VAC intervention but if there were any current concerns they would discuss it. It was very clear to me that we had a system in place that you are not meant to challenge. You are just meant to lie down and take whatever is thrown at you and to be grateful for any support or help you do receive, regardless of its quality or relevance in the context of caring for someone. Nevertheless, I was determined not to lie down. I also want to mention that I sincerely believe that if the previous head of Community care (or previous team) were still in charge this would never have happened. They knew us as a family and knew Ingrid having visited her and met with and worked with us previously. I believe a thorough and fair investigation would have taken place once the nursing homes' hollow and self- preserving claims were made.

In lodging what I felt was an extremely valid complaint, the very last thing I expected to have to do was protect my own reputation and need to go to extreme lengths just to prove the management team in the Home were lying in order to protect themselves. I have no doubt my anger, frustration and ire at the situation still comes through in my words here, all those years later.

There were also some other aspects of this episode that I found particularly galling (beyond having my ability to care for my daughter questioned).

Ingrid's admittance to hospital after a seizure and the fact that the nursing home would not readmit her after the hospital discharged her in the early hours of the morning as they could not monitor her all night and were unable to place a staff member in her room for a full night, despite the fact that they were being paid for 24/7 care by the HSE. When Ingrid was at home after we took her out of the nursing home (or after she was asked to leave, depending on which way you want to look at it), the HSE offered to provide 2 hours daily of care at home during office hours only although if she stayed in a nursing home they would cover the full cost, which was obviously not 24/7 care as outlined above but was still far more costly than 2 hours per day 5 days of the week for someone to visit and provide assistance in the home.

In a letter of complaint to HSE I highlighted just how hands-on I remained despite the care home being paid for full-time care of my daughter.

"During her stay there we had her home 233 days of which she stayed overnight 87 nights and four nights in WRH. From 22nd August 2008 - 25th March 2009 I catheterised Ingrid and got her to bed at the care home for 93 nights. On the days we took Ingrid home in the morning I would have to catheterise her before we left the care home.

I spoke on RTE's radio show Liveline with Joe Duffy and spoke about it publicly. I had heard a woman on the show talking about how she had been wronged, how someone said something about her that was completely untrue, and other people took it as fact. That resonated with me and I used Joe Duffy as an outlet for my frustration and anger.

When the notes were released to me (after I had requested them under the FOI Act), I found that the Ombudsman had to see five drafts of a letter of apology before it made it to me but finally, I did receive my apology from the HSE Community Care. I honestly feel like framing it!

I was both relieved and happy to finally bring the trauma of this whole episode to some sort of conclusion.

This wasn't the only time I felt myself questioned and I do want to highlight another episode later, when a wholly different can of worms was opened, one which I had hoped was long closed. After the court settlement in 2009, Ingrid had to become a ward of the court.

This involved various procedures, including a psychological assessment. We did not want to send Ingrid to a Hospital ward to be assessed, so they sent a psychiatrist to our home to assess her. We always tried to ensure Ingrid was in her home, where she felt safe and comforted, any time she had to undergo anything like this, as happened sometimes. Legally, as a ward of the court, her funds also had to be lodged with the court, who then looked after her finances. As such, I was the committee appointed by the President of the High Court acting in Ingrid's best interests on their behalf by overseeing the administering of these funds. This process was working out very well, and the staff at the court were delighted with how I handled the situation.

The staff was always lovely towards me, up until 2018 when Ingrid had to undergo a full left breast mastectomy operation. It was a hugely stressful time and a very private matter for our family. The surgery fell the day after Ingrid's 48 birthday in September. The surgeon was amazing. So risky was the operation that the nurses told me that they had orders from high authority that I was to come into the room while Ingrid was anaesthetised so that my voice would be the last she heard before the operation.

However, true to form, Ingrid came through yet another medical ordeal.

It was January 2019 by the time I was in touch with the court with my regular invoices. One day, a gentleman assistant registrar phoned me. He had taken over from the lady I had been used to.

He asked how Ingrid was. I said that all things considered, and having undergone gruelling surgery, she was doing pretty well.

What followed shocked me to the core. He asked, "Mrs Walsh, did you get permission in writing from the court for an anaesthetic to be administered to Ingrid prior to her operation?"

I was horrified. I did not know that I was expected to get permission for this. To add insult to injury, this guy then repeated his question, "Did your daughter get anaesthetic, Mrs Walsh?" I could not believe my ears, , I sharply replied, "Well, of course, she did! She had a mastectomy, for goodness sake. What absurd sort of a question is that to ask?"

He told me that as a ward of the court, it is the law that we get written permission from the court for Ingrid to receive an anaesthetic. I told him I was completely unaware of any rule of the sort. He went on to suggest I was maybe getting forgetful in my old age! I told him there was not a chance of that with the memory I had! He then said it was maybe time to get someone younger to take over Ingrid's affairs. I didn't necessarily have a problem with this and had in fact already started the process of adding Gordon, Ingrid's younger brother to the committee.

The phone call ended somehow, and he then consulted with the Professor who operated on Ingrid on the matter. I was mortified and dreaded facing him after that. It looked like I was incompetent and didn't know what I was doing. Yet, the truth was, I had never heard of this rule. Thankfully, when I spoke to the Professor, he believed everything I said and reassured me that he would deal with it. When I went back to him with Ingrid and apologised in person to him, his words were, "Mary, I sent a letter to the President of the High Court and put that to bed, and I ask you to do likewise." As it transpired, the court was meant to send me out a book detailing these rules and procedures.

When I finally received the book from two sources, I discovered that being a ward of the court meant that we had to ask the court's permission if we wanted to take Ingrid out of the country, if she wanted to get married and also if she needed general anaesthetic.

I had no clue when Ingrid was made a ward of the court that all of these laws applied. The court was even in charge of any personal savings she had.

15 - CANCER, COURAGE, CROSSES

By April 2019, I knew Ingrid didn't have long left. Ingrid never spoke like she knew she was dying, and we never told her she was dying.

We were due to see an oncologist that I had heard was a very straight-talking, no-nonsense sort of a person. I did not want her telling Ingrid that she was dying. By chance Ingrid's neurologist contacted me, and I expressed my concerns. He said to leave it with him.

Well, we walked into that lady's room the next morning, and she couldn't have been lovelier or any more discreet. She made such a fuss of Ingrid, telling her she had heard so much about her from Dr Donoghue and Dr Crowley. It turned out that Ingrid and the oncologist's birthdays were just a day apart, which pleased Ingrid no end.

When the Oncologist had finished with Ingrid I left her out to Sarah, the nurse who had come with us. Then without any drama or tears, I simply asked her, "Look me in the eye and tell me the worst-case scenario.

"I might fall apart when I get home, but I am not going to crumble at your feet here and now."

The oncologist told me Ingrid might have a couple of months left. The first person I told that her cancer had returned and she was dying was Fr Liddane, when he called that evening, and even then, I just gave him the notes the oncologist had written rather than let the words come out of my mouth. It wasn't until after she had a massive seizure during the night that I told Ernie at 4 a.m. that she was dying.

The week after the oncologist spoke with me the Palliative care team came on board. They called every week to check on Ingrid and have a chat. They then came more often and stayed overnight for the last two nights of Ingrid's life. They were wonderful. As a family we were all here at the end. They kept us informed and were very supportive.

Another very special friend whom I confided in was Sister Moya, who is based in Sligo. She travelled to visit Ingrid in the months before her death. I was making lunch while Ingrid and Moya were in the sitting room of Ingrid's house. I went to call them for lunch only to find Moya removing her beautiful chain and cross from around her neck. I asked her what she was doing, and she said, "I'm giving it to Ingrid. She admired it, and I would like her to have it." I tried to stop her, but she was insistent. It was a beautiful piece, and even though Ingrid had never been into jewellery her whole life, she wore that chain and cross constantly.

One of the nurses looking after Ingrid at the time admired it one evening and joked that Ingrid had no sister and she should leave it to her in her will. Directly, matter- of-factly, Ingrid took one look at her and said, "Why would I be doing such a thing when I have a sister-in-law (Nichola) of my own to give it to". After Ingrid's death I tried to return that cross to Sr. Moya. No way would she take it, "It was Ingrid's wish that Nichola would get it," she said. And that's who got the cross and chain. It was with Ingrid in her wicker casket right up until the lid went on. It was then given to her sister-in-law and best friend, Nichola. Nichola was delighted to receive it. Despite being so ill, Ingrid continued to bring people together. In what turned out to be her final weeks on this earth, she was rarely without visitors. Bill Curtin, a family friend, was one of the last non family people to visit Ingrid. He used to take Ingrid out for afternoon tea when she was well and told me often how much he 'just loved her company.' Bill owned several factories and once took Ingrid to one of them and asked her to design a mirror. Well, Ingrid was in her element. She loved art and design. Bill took her mirror design and manufactured it, and it hangs in our home to this day as a fitting reminder of how gifted and loved Ingrid was.

On Sunday 16th June when our good nursing nun friend Sr. Francis was leaving Ingrid put out her hand to her, saying "I want to thank you for caring."

On Monday 17th June Ingrid's final week with us, Isobel Ingrid's first cousin and constant visitor visited. She knelt down beside Ingrid's bed. Ingrid put her hand on Isobel's shoulder tapping it and said, "Bel we had fun and thank you, thank you!" On the Tuesday night 18th June when the nurse came on duty, I went to say good night to Ingrid. She put her hands locked tightly around my neck and said these words I will never ever forget, "Mam I want to say to you that you and Dad have been the best parents the world over. I want to tell you how much I love you and thank you and hope I wasn't too much of a bother." I am one good at hiding my emotions but not that night. The tears flowed. I did my best to tell Ingrid she was the best that ever happened to her Dad and I and we wouldn't have been without any of it. Even in the last days of her life, true to character, as we tried to protect Ingrid, she was busy protecting everyone around her.

In those final days I would ask Ingrid what her pain was like on a scale of 1 to 10. By Wednesday when I asked she replied, "Mam it's over 100 now." That's when the syringe driver went in. The last thing Ingrid ever ate was a piece of coffee cake.

On the rare occasions when Ingrid managed not to speak her mind, her true feelings were always written all over her face. Marie Kavanagh, a professional teacher of flower arranging, knows this all too well. Marie always brought Ingrid a beautiful fresh flower arrangement for her birthday. A few years before Ingrid died, Marie came with the most stunning dried flower arrangement for her. Ingrid's face fell, and her eyes lowered. She was not impressed. She adored fresh flowers but had no place in her heart for dried ones. Ingrid was too polite to say anything to Marie, but she only had to look at Ingrid's disappointed eyes to know. Marie came back with beautiful fresh flowers and the joy on Ingrid's face and in her eyes said it all.

Father's Day came on 16th June 2019, and ever- thoughtful Ingrid filled in the card for her dad and gave him his favourite homemade chocolates. Gordon was also in the room, and she even remembered to wish him a very happy first Father's Day.

Little did we know then that the following Sunday we would be attending Ingrid's funeral.

We had been told so many times over the years that Ingrid probably won't be there in the morning. But every single time she made it; she was always there... until one day she wasn't. That day came on Friday 21st June when I had a gut feeling around 6 a.m., and I got up and made myself a cup of tea.

I was going to go and take a shower but decided against it and instead went and sat with Ingrid. I had noticed that a slight change had come over her face and she looked like a porcelain doll. I sat there talking to her about all those that would be waiting for her.

With a deep quiet breath in, she left this earth. Her exit was so calm. So tranquil. I was the only person with her when she died, and I feel so blessed about that.

From Wednesday to Friday, I prayed harder than anyone could ever know that Ingrid wouldn't have a long-drawn- out painful death. And she certainly didn't. Ingrid had a lovely death, exactly what she deserved.

Ingrid wasn't into drama and she certainly left this earth with none whatsoever. She left it looking out on a fabulous garden in full bloom. I sat by her side after she had gone silently drinking in the garden's vibrant colours and I felt totally at peace.

I honestly have the happiest memories of that day and afterwards when she was laid out, and everyone who loved her came to see her. Lying there on her side, in her wicker coffin, she looked like she was just sleeping. Everyone felt like if you gave her a dig, she would wake up and speak to you. If only!

Ingrid never touched alcohol or cigarettes, but she had a sweet tooth. She loved and enjoyed chocolate. There was always a huge volume of Easter eggs to be opened on Easter Sunday, as everyone knew how much she enjoyed her chocolate with a cup of tea. She loved coffee cake and it was the last thing she ever had to eat. It was incredible to see the volume of coffee cakes handed in for her wake by friends and neighbours. I think I remember counting 13. The goodness and kindness of neighbours and everyone who knew Ingrid was remarkable.

Ingrid's brother Gordon wrote the eulogy for Ingrid's funeral. I am including it in full here because it is beautifully written. I don't believe anyone could have summed Ingrid up any more perfectly.

When he read it, everyone in the church was in tears, smiling and applauding all at the same time because it came directly from the heart of a bereft brother who was saying goodbye to his best friend. Gordon wrote the eulogy while spending his last bit of quality time with Ingrid the night before her funeral. His words were inspired by all the memories that came flooding back and also by all the treasured memorabilia around Ingrid's room.

Reader, if you never knew Ingrid, let Gordon's words paint you a perfect picture of her...

INGRID'S EULOGY BY GORDON

I learnt more from my big sister than I can ever describe or probably than I will ever realise.

I learnt how to walk by doing circles around her wheelchair, and I learnt how to climb by clambering up her chair to use that as a springboard to get to higher shelves. Many times I did that at Ingrid's instruction because the chocolates or 'good biscuits' were hidden away on the top shelf.

I learnt humility, empathy and decency before I even knew what any of those meant. Ingrid's reaction to my being born was to say, "Isn't it wonderful that he's going to be able to walk!"

Ingrid didn't do bitterness or recriminations, and she certainly didn't believe in the impossible. She loved life and loved living – she fought hard enough to be here on so many occasions that she was determined to enjoy life as much as she possibly could. She loved informing everyone that the doctors told her on day one that she wouldn't make it, but she proved them all wrong. She's often added that the majority were only professors, and what do they know anyway!

She loved fighting expectations and defying any reasonable odds. Ingrid always had a smile and a kind word for everyone and would always answer a question about her own health, retorting, "But more importantly, how are you?" And she really meant it too – she wasn't interested in talking about her own pain or misfortune, just wanted to focus on others and on what was positive.

She had such a massively positive effect on the lives of so many people, and I can see from yesterday and today still has an amazing ability to bring people together, which will be a huge part of Ingrid's memory and her legacy. She was generous to a fault and took more joy from giving to others than anything else.

Many of the happiest memories of Ingrid involve her and Graham listening to music together and introducing me (or at least trying) to the Boomtown Rats and Queen.

I wouldn't realise until I was much older just how great their taste in music really was. She would appreciate the fact that her funeral is today and not tomorrow, given that her favourite song was, 'I don't like Mondays'.

She loved spending time with Graham and his friends – was always delighted and proud to spend time with her older brother, and he loved showing off his baby sister too, whether it was by carrying her up the stairs into the cinema or keeping her on his shoulders for the day during Lark in the Park here in Waterford.

She loved art and painting and learning new things and was very creative. She was so proud of all the things that Dad built for her throughout the years to enable her to live as full a life as possible. She even spent quite a bit of time with him listening to classical music as she got older, although he's still no fan of the Boomtown Rats.

Ingrid was the teenager who, after waiting months for a new wheelchair, sent it straight back to the Health Board because it was turquoise. It was too bright; Ingrid only wanted a black wheelchair because, as far as she was concerned, it was up to her to bring the colour. She wanted to make sure that people saw her first and the chair afterwards.

She was the young girl who toured schools talking about her experience as a wheelchair user, dealing with disability and other people's reactions. She loved her independence to such an extent that Ingrid would never even allow anyone else to pour milk in her tea for her.

Ingrid was never able to stand up but was determined to stand out. She has been on Nationwide, met with the President and Taoiseach (and of course Phil Coulter), is on first name terms with two Bishops and never had an encounter with anyone who didn't feel enriched by her company and her essence. Everyone loved Ingrid for exactly who she was.

Although she didn't have a long time with him, she was an amazing aunt to Luke, and we'll always cherish those few months she got to spend doting on him. Ingrid was an incredible sister, a wonderful daughter and the best friend anyone could ever ask for.

Ingrid would want me to say a huge thank you to Father Liddane for all his visits in the past week and the past number of weeks and months. She loved seeing him arrive at our house and his kindness and compassion were a great source of comfort to Ingrid and to the whole family.

Just finally, Ingrid wouldn't want me to step down from here without saying a final thank you.

A definition of the name 'Ingrid' has been hanging on the wall of her bedroom since Christmas 1995 when Mam and Dad gave her a framed present of it. [Included on page 14] The name is of Norse origin and it actually means 'Hero's Daughter', which is very appropriate and poignant because Ingrid would want me to use her voice today to say a massive, heartfelt, thank you to our parents for all the love and care they gave to her and for ensuring that her quality of life was incredible right until the end. In the face of such illness and odds, she was eternally grateful for the parents she had. She received infinite amounts of love and support, whether it was through Dad making toys, chairs and contraptions for her as a child and adolescent or Mam fighting a lengthy battle that she could no longer fight herself in the courts. They were always immensely proud of her, and being able to ultimately pass on her own terms in the home where she lived all her life was as it should be.

It was very fitting that Ingrid was at home until the very end and that the last voice she heard was Mam's. That is exactly what Ingrid would have wanted.

When she was seven weeks old, our parents drove her home from hospital in Dublin with instructions to return in six weeks' time if she was still alive. The conversation in the car was about how they were going to cope, and Dad simply said, "We'll love her as much as we can for as long as we can." And they certainly did that.

I want to finish with someone else's words and a message that really encapsulates Ingrid. She would also approve of it, given it has been hanging on the wall in her home for many years.

Invictus

Out of the night that covers me,
Black as the pit from pole to pole,
I thank whatever gods may be
For my unconquerable soul.

In the fell clutch of circumstance
I have not winced nor cried aloud.
Under the bludgeonings of chance
My head is bloody, but unbowed.

Beyond this place of wrath and tears
Looms but the Horror of the shade,
And yet the menace of the years
Finds, and shall find, me unafraid.

It matters not how strait the gate,
How charged with punishments the scroll,
I am the master of my fate: I am the captain of my soul.

By William Ernest Henley

Sleep well, Ingrid.

OUR HEROINE

As Gordon said in his eulogy, Ingrid passed on her own terms. The last voice she heard was mine, and she died in her beloved happy place, her home.

Ingrid's was the most beautiful corpse I have ever laid eyes on. She looked comfortable in her wicker casket. There was no way our girl would be put to 'rest' in a hard wooden one. She was on her side, of course. She had never lain on her back in her life, so there was no way she was going to lie on it now.

As in life, so in death, Ingrid brought many people together. Hundreds of people passed through our home to pay their respects. I often think if you could bottle the essence of Ingrid and sell it, you'd be a rich woman, and the world would be an enriched place for it.

Fr Liddane, whose visits Ingrid took great comfort from in her final days, so accurately described her at the funeral. "That smile... her eyes just lit up... she was so genuine."

Prof. Guiney died the same year as Ingrid, but I didn't tell her. It seemed somewhat fitting that the man who gave Ingrid a chance at life was now with her in another life.

As for Dr. Paul Crowley, Neurologist, Prof. Gerry O'Donoghue, surgeon, Mr. Steven Young, neurosurgeon and Dr. Miriam

O'Connor oncologist I will be eternally grateful to each and every one of these wonderful human beings. They remained devoted to providing Ingrid with the very best level of care, while others fell very short of their impeccable standards.

I meet people daily who miss her terribly. What do they miss about her? It would be easier to answer what they don't miss about her. They miss everything about her... her smile, her laugh, her hugs, her wit, her talent, her wisdom, her advice, her patience, her empathy, her decency and her humility.

The person who existed to bring people together may have physically gone, but her memory and legacy are so strong that I know people will always gather to speak about her.

To this day, I have nurses calling to visit me and reminisce about their precious Ingrid, whom they got the pleasure of nursing. Ingrid's very good friend Aine from Australia was just here visiting recently, and we reminisced about the fun those two girls had, especially when Aine looked after Ingrid while Ernie and I went on holiday. Aine and Ingrid became friends in St. Paul's College and remained friends. When Aine went working and met Richard who later became her husband, they often took Ingrid out to different events. Ingrid was so pleased to attend their wedding.

I am dedicating this book to Ingrid's niece and nephew. Luke, whom she got the opportunity to meet and love, and Ava

Ingrid, who was born one year after her aunt and namesake's death.

Just the other Friday, during my traditional live video sessions with my grandchildren in Dublin, I watched as Luke laid a little rug down on the floor as a 'magic carpet' for his baby sister Ava to fly on. Well, this made my heart soar as it reminded me of Ingrid sailing around the nursery on her magic carpet. Luke has also been given some of Ingrid's toys that I had kept, one of them her very first Christmas present, a Fisher-Price clock that looks its age now!

I hope in time, Luke and Ava will read Ingrid's story, be inspired by it and share it with their own children.

The light that Ingrid shone on this world cannot be extinguished for as long as her bright, colourful story remains.

Dear reader, next time you get the pleasure of meeting talented and inspirational people who happen to be in a wheelchair, please think of my independent, defiant Ingrid. Please don't discriminate or patronise them. You could regret it. They could have a tongue as sharp and a wit as quick as Ingrid's!

Be inspired by Ingrid's story like we all have been. Her desire for people to always see her before her wheelchair has certainly resonated with and inspired Gordon: after his kids arrived, he told me that he would always make sure they are taught to look beyond a wheelchair or any physical disabilities that people may have. His tactic with his kids has been to draw their attention to something else, like a lovely bow in a girl's hair or a nice t-shirt or bright shoes that a boy is wearing, rather than focus on the wheelchair first. The idea is for his kids to notice and appreciate something else entirely and the hope is that they never even become aware of any disability.

I received a letter recently from a school friend of Ingrid's that simply said, "Aww Mary, a bubbly and smiley individual she was!" That is what people saw. Not poor Ingrid in her wheelchair because Ingrid never behaved like poor Ingrid in her wheelchair. Ingrid was never treated differently by her friends because she didn't act differently. Never once in all her years did Ingrid say, "Why me?" or "Poor me."

Ingrid's room sits much the same as it did with all her fluffy teddies on the wall. Ernie and I did go to her room on the day after her burial and just held each other. It was an eerie feeling, but if we had put it off, it would have been harder.

If I go there now to remember her, I go alone, because my rock, my constant, my Ernie went to be with Ingrid just two years after her death. I have a photo that I often look at when I miss them both. It sums them up perfectly. There they are, together, and Ingrid has her arm up, ready to give her dad a dig in the ribs for a laugh. Their relationship was so special. They had such a laugh together, always winding each other up. She would sit listening to classical music with him. She would do out menus for him to cook. The banter between them was constant. It was something else, just magic.

I also have their graves to visit, both with a photograph of them and the beautiful inscription on the headstone saying "To have died so dearly loved is not to have lived in vain." This is so true. Even visitors stumbling across them will see how special they were on this earth.

I know there are people who visit that grave that I have never met, people that Ingrid touched. One day when I visited, I found Bill and Angela Curtin there. It was so lovely to see them and reminisce about Ingrid. Had I not bumped into them that day, I would never have known they had been there. I'm sure there are many others that I am not aware of.

I'm not ready to give up my titles of 'Ernie's Mary' or 'Ingrid's mam' just yet. I'm too proud of them. I saw Dr Liam McCann again recently. He called me 'Ernie's Mary' and in conversation said about Ingrid, "Wasn't she something else, Mary? She was."

My brother Kevin, Ingrid's uncle, was so impacted by Ingrid's death he was inspired to write a beautiful poem:

INGRID

On broken wing, you went through life
Body racked but with a smiling face
Mountains, rivers and tidal waves
Faith tossed them into your race.
Never one to shirk a challenge
You mustered all your strength
Dug deep within your mental core
Facing all with dignity and stealth.
The battle continued to rage for you
Life's salvos came hard and fast
Withstanding all that life could throw
Loved ones wondered if each was the last.
Life took a heavy toll on you
It was difficult to win every fight
And with the final counterattack
Armoury depleted, bid all goodnight.
The good die young they tell us
For you, this is surely so
Those left behind are empty
Full of sadness and full of woe.
I see you now where eagles soar
A dove among cumulus clouds
Your wing no longer broken
Perched high and looking proud.

By Kevin Douglas, Uncle

I am trying very hard to adjust to my life without my husband, the love of my life, who was described the other day as "A unique, talented, exceptional man." The support since I said goodbye to Ingrid and Ernie has been amazing. Almost every day, I'm reminded of how exceptional they both were.

I met a man as I was sanitising my hands in SuperValu recently, and he announced that Ernie had given him his first week's wages and taught him how to drive. He continued,

"He really loved you, Mary! He taught me a lot about love." Then he told this story,

"Ernie was making a stool for you in the workshop because you'd had a disc operation on your back or something, and us men were all joking with him saying things like, "Is that for the one you kneel to for adoration?" Well, as quick and direct as you like, Ernie looked us eejits in the eyes and said proudly, "Well you got that right, first time!"

I spoke recently to one of the wonderful nurses who cared for Ingrid towards the end of her life. To mark her retirement, she met up with some of the other nurses who had also worked with Ingrid. She lauded me with praise while I blushed at the other end of the phone. She told me, "You were very much the subject of conversation when we got together, Mary. I don't think you have any inkling just how big an impact you made on our lives. You taught us so much about caring that we could never have learnt from a textbook. We were all remembering just how you were able to make the best of a bad situation time and time again!"

Breda O'Brien, another extra special lady who was so inspired by Ingrid that she spent years tirelessly raising huge amounts of money for Crumlin Hospital in thanksgiving for keeping Ingrid alive, she got in touch recently to say the most heart-warming things. "Mary, it never ceased to amaze me when I was in your home that nothing seemed a bother. You made it look so easy, but Mary, I know it couldn't have been easy!"

Breda was right, it was far from easy, but we were a family that didn't wear our problems on our faces. For as long as we still had Ingrid, just as Ernie had said all those years ago, we would continue to love and cherish her. This meant not worrying Ingrid with our worries, not upsetting Ingrid with our frustrations and not sacrificing one day when we could still laugh instead of wasting our precious time on negative emotions. Breda's latest fundraising event for Crumlin was her marathon in New York over St. Patrick's weekend.

Despite Ernie and Ingrid having gone physically from this world, I still try not to cave into bitterness, anger or despair. Yes, I have moments of deep, deep sadness when I cry, and I hurt because I miss them so much, but I don't let the ugly feelings take hold. When they encroach, I think of Ingrid's huge smile and bright eyes, and I always, always replace the bad with the good times.

And so, I remain here on earth, 'Ernie's Mary' and 'Ingrid's mam,' with my two angels by my side guiding every word I write and digging me in the ribs when I get too sad or telling me to go and play solitaire.

I miss you both so much, my beloved Ingrid and my one true love, Ernie.

I promise you, Ingrid, every single time I see a thing of colour in this world, there you will be.

Nichola's trip to meet Ingrid, and the cross and chain Ingrid bequeathed to Nichola

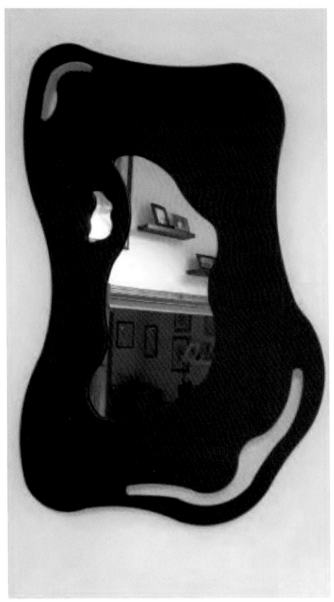

This was a mirror designed by Ingrid and manufactured by Bill - a unique heirloom

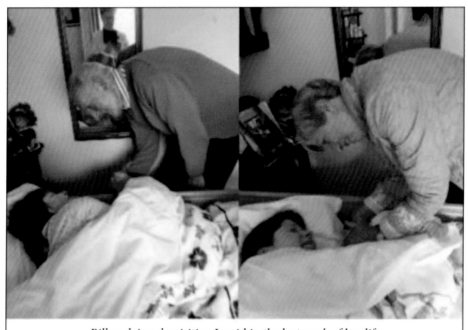

Bill and Angela visiting Ingrid in the last week of her life

*Breda O'Brien after completing the marathon in NY, raising money for
Our Lady's Hospital, Crumlin on behalf of Ingrid*

Ingrid and Breda together

*Ingrid, Gordon and Nichola with Nichola's parents on one of
their many visits to see Ingrid*

Sisters Francis and Columba with Ingrid and her dad

Ingrid as Batman and Aine as The Joker for Aoife McCann's 21st birthday

Ingrid with Aine

Ingrid greeting President Mary McAleese

Ingrid meeting Bertie Ahern, then Taoiseach

Sunday, 16th June - Ingrid and her dad together on Father's Day

GLOSSARY

Atrium - The two atria are thin-walled chambers that receive blood from the veins. The two ventricles are thick-walled chambers that forcefully pump blood out of the heart.

Barium enema - A barium enema is a test that helps to highlight the large bowel so it can be clearly seen on an X-ray. During the test, a white liquid called barium is passed into your bowel through your bottom. A barium enema may be requested by any doctor who thinks you might have a problem with your bowel, including your GP.

Cerebrospinal fluid – Cerebrospinal fluid (CSF) is a clear, colourless liquid found in your brain and spinal cord. The brain and spinal cord make up your central nervous system. Your central nervous system controls and coordinates everything you do including, muscle movement, organ function, and even complex thinking and planning.

Forceps delivery - A forceps delivery is a type of assisted vaginal delivery. It's sometimes needed in the course of vaginal childbirth. In a forceps delivery, a health care provider applies forceps — an instrument shaped like a pair of large spoons or salad tongs — to the baby's head to help guide the baby out of the birth canal.

GI Colleagues - A GI doctor, also known as a Gastroenterologist, is a medical doctor with special training in the diagnosis and treatment of diseases affecting the digestive tract.

Haemoglobin levels - The haemoglobin count is an indirect measurement of the number of red blood cells in your body. When the haemoglobin count is higher than normal, it may be a sign of a health problem. Normal haemoglobin counts are 14 to 17 gm/dL (grams per decilitre) for men and 12 to 15 gm/dL for women.

Hydrocephalus - Hydrocephalus is a build-up of fluid in the brain. The excess fluid puts pressure on the brain, which can damage it. If left untreated, hydrocephalus can be fatal.

Hypo chromic microcytic anaemia - Microcytic, hypochromic anaemia, as the name suggests, is the type of anaemia in which the circulating RBCs are smaller than the usual size of RBCs (microcytic) and have decreased red colour (hypochromic).

Nodular epic scleritis - Nodular scleritis is an inflammatory condition affecting the sclera that is often associated with underlying systemic collagen vascular disease, vasculitis, or other auto-immune disease. Nodular scleritis causes severe injection and pain in an elevated area (or nodule) of the sclera.

Peritoneum - The peritoneum is the serous membrane forming the lining of the abdominal cavity or coelom in amniotes and some invertebrates, such as annelids. It covers most of the intra-abdominal (or coelomic) organs, and is composed of a layer of mesothelium supported by a thin layer of connective tissue.

Positive rheumatoid factor - A positive rheumatoid factor test result indicates that a high level of rheumatoid factor was detected in your blood. A higher level of rheumatoid factor in your blood is closely associated with autoimmune disease, particularly rheumatoid arthritis.

Reiter's Syndrome - Reiter's syndrome is a form of arthritis that produces pain swelling redness and heat in the joints. It is one of a family of arthritic disorders affecting the spine. Reiter's commonly involves the joints of the spine and the sacroiliac joints areas where the spine attaches to the pelvis.

SHO - A senior house officer (SHO) is a non-consultant hospital doctor in the Republic of Ireland. SHOs are supervised in their work by consultants and registrars.

Shunt - A shunt is a hollow tube surgically placed in the brain (or occasionally in the spine) to help drain cerebrospinal fluid and redirect it to another location in the body where it can be reabsorbed.

Spinal osteotomy - Spine osteotomy is a surgical procedure in which a section of the spinal bone is cut and removed to allow for correction of spinal alignment.

A Spitz-Holter valve - A one-way valve used to drain cerebrospinal fluid in order to control hydrocephalus. The device is inserted into the ventricles of the brain and passes via a subcutaneous tunnel to drain into either the right atrium or the peritoneum.

Tonic colonic seizure - A tonic-colonic seizure is what most people think of when they think of a seizure. · Another word for this is a convulsion.

Upper GI endoscopy - An upper GI endoscopy or EGD (esophagogastroduodenoscopy) is a procedure to diagnose and treat problems in your upper GI (gastrointestinal) tract. The upper GI tract includes your food pipe (oesophagus), stomach, and the first part of your small intestine (the duodenum).

Valve tap – Valve tap or shunt tap is when fluid is taken from the shunt for analysis when an infection or blockage is suspected.

Ventricles - A ventricle is one of two large chambers toward the bottom of the heart that collect and expel blood towards the peripheral beds within the body and lungs. The blood pumped by a ventricle is supplied by an atrium, an adjacent chamber in the upper heart that is smaller than a ventricle.

Ingrid and her dad having banter

Ingrid and Mary together at Lourdes